"Compelling"
—NEWSWEEK

"Moves the reader, not just emotionally, but intellectually, and in startling new directions . . . Astonishing . . . This is a good book, which should be read."
—NEW YORK TIMES REVIEW OF BOOKS

"She tells her story with austere and impressive eloquence . . . Extraordinary."
—KIRKUS REVIEWS

"It is a sad story, yet the sadness is not what sticks with you at its end; what is most impressive is, rather, the resilience and tenacity of a woman whose reserves of strengths have enabled her to withstand losses that would have destroyed lesser people."
—WASHINGTON POST BOOK WORLD

"Vivid, immediate, and occasionally harrowing . . . A genuine talent."
—BOSTON SUNDAY GLOBE

"Fascinating . . . A significant book well worth reading."
—DAVID HARTMAN
GOOD MORNING AMERICA

"Startling . . . Ranks among the best, most vivid and illuminating prison writing I have read."
—SUSAN BROWNMILLER
CHICAGO TRIBUNE BOOKWORLD

"Passionate . . . Well-written . . . Powerful"
—CLEVELAND PLAIN DEALER

"(Harris) is an accomplished writer with a fine ear for dialogue . . . An eloquent work about the waste of life and spirit in prison."
—WALL STREET JOURNAL

"A thoughtful, balanced and surprisingly unself-pitying account of a life that went disastrously adrift"
—PETER L. ROBERTSON
AMERICAN LIBRARY ASSN.

"Riveting . . . A moving and eloquent account by a woman of extraordinary intelligence . . . A superb book . . . Harris writes passionately and powerfully . . . A triumphant release."
—SAN FRANCISCO CHRONICLE

"A deeply generous and intelligent book that will make you—like Jean Harris herself—see things differently than you did before."
—NEW YORK NEWSDAY

P9-DXT-269

YOUR FAVORITE CELEBRITIES
From Zebra Books

STRANGER IN TWO WORLDS   (2112, $4.50)
by Jean Harris
For the first time, the woman convicted in the shooting death of
Scarsdale Diet Doctor Herman Tarnower tells her own story. Here
is the powerful and compelling truth of the love affair and its
shocking aftermath.

STOCKMAN: THE MAN, THE MYTH,
THE FUTURE   (2005, $4.50)
by Owen Ullmann
As director of the Office of Management & Budget, Stockman
was the youngest man to sit at the Cabinet in more than 160
years. Here is the first full-scale, objective, no-holds-barred story
of Ronald Reagan's most controversial advisor, David Stockman.

DUKE: THE LIFE AND TIMES OF
JOHN WAYNE   (1935, $3.95)
by Donald Shepherd & Robert Slatzer with Dave Grayson
From his childhood as the son of a failed druggist to his gallant
battle against cancer, here's what the "Duke" was really like — with
all the faults that made him human and all the courage and honesty that made him one of Hollywood's greatest and most endearing stars.

IACOCCA   (1700, $3.95)
by David Abodaher
As president of Ford and father of the Mustang, Iacocca's been a
force to be reckoned with in the car industry for two decades. But
it was due to his inexplicable fall from grace with Henry Ford that
Iacocca took on the Chrysler challenge. By turning that dying
corporation around through sheer will power and pull in the biggest profits in Chrysler's hisotry, the respected business leader became a modern-day folk hero.

*Available wherever paperbacks are sold, or order direct from the
Publisher. Send cover price plus 50¢ per copy for mailing and
handling to Zebra Books, Dept. 2112, 475 Park Avenue South,
New York, N.Y. 10016. Residents of New York, New Jersey and
Pennsylvania must include sales tax. DO NOT SEND CASH.*

JEAN HARRIS

STRANGER IN TWO WORLDS

All of the Author's profits from
this book have been assigned
by her to <u>Children of Bedford</u>,
a charitable corporation.

ZEBRA BOOKS
KENSINGTON PUBLISHING CORP.

ZEBRA BOOKS

are published by

Kensington Publishing Corp.
475 Park Avenue South
New York, NY 10016

Copyright © 1986 by Jean Harris. Reprinted by arrangement with Macmillan Publishing Company.

All rights reserved. No part of this book may be reproduced in any form or by any means without the prior written consent of the Publisher, excepting brief quotes used in reviews.

First Zebra Books Printing: July 1987

Printed in the United States of America

Grateful acknowledgment is made to the following for permission to reprint previously published material from:
   The Joke by Milan Kundera, translated by Michael Henry Heim. English translation copyright © 1982 by Harper & Row, Publishers, Inc. Original title *Zert* copyright © 1967 by Milan Kundera. By permission of Harper & Row, Publishers, Inc.
   Collected Poems by Edna St. Vincent Millay, Harper & Row, Publishers, Inc. Copyright © 1923, 1931, 1951, 1958 by Edna St. Vincent Millay and Norma Millay Ellis.
   Man's Search for Meaning by Viktor Frankl, Beacon Press. Copyright © 1962 by Viktor Frankl. By permission of Beacon Press.
   "The Physician as Expert Witness" by A. Bernard Ackerman, M.D., *Medical Heritage*. By permission of A. Bernard Ackerman and W.B. Saunders Co.

Photo credits appear on page 551.

This book is for my sons,
David Michael Harris, and James Scholes Harris, Jr.,
with my love.

Contents

"I beseech ye in the bowels of Christ, think that ye may be mistaken." I should like to have that written over the portals of every church, every school, and every courthouse, and may I say of every legislative body in the United States. I should like to have every court begin, *"I beseech ye in the bowels of Christ, think that we may be mistaken."*

Judge Learned Hand

Acknowledgments

The many kindnesses that have been shown me over the past six years are beyond anything I could have imagined. Thousands of people from all over America, and all over the world, have written, wishing me well. I'm happy to say their letters will become part of the archives of Smith College. I hope that someday a young graduate student will read them, and find in them a piece of Americana, proof positive that in spite of what has happened to me, there was goodness abroad in the land.

That I am here is not because many good people have not wished and worked and prayed to have me free. They have bestowed upon me love and trust, and given their time and energy, and patience, and understanding and expertise, and money in my behalf. I am proud to call each one friend.

The list that follows cannot be complete. It would be too long. To each of you who has smiled and reached out a hand I am deeply grateful. Your

9

kindnesses have spilled over into the lives of many other women here, as well as into mine.

My special appreciation and deep affection go to Sister Elaine Roulet, Arlene Levkoff, and William Riegelman, three very dear human beings who unquestionably have helped me to retain my sanity in this grim, terrible place. Sister Elaine is head of the Children's Center where I work here at Bedford Hills Correctional Facility, a top security prison for women in the State of New York. At the risk of not making life easier for her by having me sing her praises, there is no way to tell of my life in prison without saying how deeply I admire her and how grateful I am that she is here. I think all of us who work closely with her share this feeling. The days she isn't here are colorless and dull. She brings life and humor and a sense of purpose into our lives.

Bill Riegelman was a virtual stranger to me the night Hy died. He was called in the middle of the night to come and help me until others could arrive. He was there beside me in a tiny room in a Westchester jail when a policeman told me in a casual voice: "Dr. Herman Tarnower? Oh, he passed on." He was there beside me for the next three years, until his own death. He cheered me in every way he could, and kept me informed about what was happening in my case when others were too busy. He handled my private legal matters for me, without being asked and without ever sending a bill. I said to him one day, "I figure on an hourly basis I must owe you about two million dollars by now. Do you want to flip, double or nothing?" he laughed and said, "You don't owe me anything." He made me laugh and he made me cry and he made me angry, and he calmed me down with, "Don't be so hyperbolic, Jean." He used to promise, "I'll live to see you out of here." I wish we

10

both could have made it.

Arlene Levkoff, over the years, has become like a daughter to me, always full of life and funny stories, and heartwarming loyalty, no matter how hard the media was beating on me. No request, however busy she may be, is too large or too small for her to run right out and fill for me. Whether it is a spool of thread and a hairnet I need, or a robe and night-gown, or toys for the Children's Center, or clothes for Sister's Thrift Shop, or Christmas shopping for David and Jim, she is always there with a smile. She has mailed endless things for me so they wouldn't sit for weeks in the prison mail room, or just disappear, and she has indulged me in charming and ridiculous and heartwarming ways. Best of all she has shared her children, Jodi and Brett, and her dearest friend, Janet Levkoff, with me. Together they have done many kindnesses for the Children's Center, and they are much loved by all of us.

My sisters, Mary Margaret Lynch and Virginia McLaughlin, and my brother Robert Struven, though living far away, have stood staunchly beside me when they could, and have been with me in spirit always, never wavering in their loyalty and offers of help.

Three kind women took me into their homes during the year after Hy died, so that I could be living, as I was ordered by the court to do, in Westchester. I lived for nine months with Frances Braxton in her wonder-ful old house by the duck pond, and came to know and love her family. She even welcomed my big, shedding, lovable golden retriever, Cider. Linda Co-hen befriended me in a hundred different ways, and it was she and Rebecca, and Matthew and Seth who bought and trimmed a Christmas tree for me that first Christmas far away from home.

Roz Riegelman's kindness helped to ease the

11

trauma and tension of those eight long days while we waited for the jury's verdict.

Shana Alexander's gifts to me are unique. I have not read her book about me. I do not wish to hear in detail what she thinks about Hy or me. It is enough to know that we are kindred souls, that she understands what makes me tick, that I trust her, and that when I call her in the middle of the night, as I sometimes have, and say, "Shana, just talk. Please, just keep talking so I'll know that something still makes sense," she will.

Sue Cullman's visits mean something special to me because she knows, perhaps better than anyone else, the hurt that I have lived through. Her kindnesses come from the heart, and in their quiet, low key way have touched the lives of every woman in here. It is in part through her generosity that I have been able to keep alive a small program for ladies in the mental ward here.

Ann Lenox, a great headmistress and a great friend, has worked long and hard to establish a defense fund in my behalf. Alice Lacey has worked beside her in this endeavor and her gifts of friendship and beautiful yarns from Hillside Farm have given pleasure not only to me but to many of the women here, and to their children.

Michael and Eleanora Kennedy are two kind and caring people who came late into my life, but thank heavens they came. Michael has exhausted every possible legal avenue for winning me a new trial, but they refuse to let me give up. If effort and selfless determination can set me free, they are the two people who will make it happen. How does one measure gratitude?

Leslie Jacobson was the lawyer I called the night Hy died. He came at once to help, and continued to help in many ways though he is not a criminal lawyer. He and his wife, Marjorie, had introduced me to Hy fourteen years earlier. My friendship with Marjorie spans almost sixty years, and many happy, funny times. I hope we will both live long enough to see so much sadness fade.

Carol Potts, the kind, competent lady who was secretary and friend to me at the Madeira School, helped me salvage needed records and papers and continues to cheer me with her visits and news of her family. Jackie Barnes, the special lady who filled the same role in Philadelphia, writes, and visits when she can, and mothers me and chides me when I don't call to tell her how I am.

Audrey and Seymour Topping have sent me my window on the world, *The New York Times*, all these years. I am deeply grateful. Sally Duncan has befriended me, and in doing so has become friend to many others here. She seems to have a sixth sense about when we need more colored felt in the Center, or magic markers, or Christmas tree ornaments, and her gifts of personal kindness to me are unnumbered.

Dr. Bernard Ackerman was one of the medical experts who gave testimony at my trial. We were strangers, but he shared with me his disbelief and disillusion at what can happen in a court of law. It was a first, for both of us. He has, at his own expense, written widely on the subject of expert testimony and the medical testimony in my trial in particular. The strength of his integrity, that rarest of all qualities, delights my soul.

Herbert MacDonnell studied the physical evidence in Hy's room far more carefully than anyone else involved in the case, and explained to the jury in clear and accurate terms what the physical evidence indicated. That they chose not to believe him is a frustra-

13

tion we share. He is kind enough to come and visit from time to time, and to express again his belief that I told the truth. It would be hard to put into words how much that means to me.

I am grateful to Mrs. Liza Zumar, a member of my jury who has written to wish me well, to tell me of the depression she felt after the trial, and who has expressed the hope publicly that I will be granted a new trial.

Laura Haywood has sent me a book almost every week for five years, among them all the works of Loren Eiseley, which I had treasured for years and hadn't hoped to see again. She has also helped me to put together a collection of studies about women in prison, published and unpublished works that have broadened my knowledge of incarcerated women far beyond the barbed wire of Bedford. These, too, are gradually going to Smith.

I have said little in this book about two lawyers who have worked in my behalf, Joel Aurnou and Herald Price Fahringer, not because I am ungrateful for their efforts. I am grateful. Both of them wanted to help me. Both of them worked hard in my behalf. Joel believed the truth would set me free, which I now know was naive in the extreme, but at the time it seemed quite logical to me. They did much to give me hope, even when there wasn't any. They were kind to me. They are, I know, sorry that I am here. What else can one say? Life goes on.

There is one other group of friends I have never met, but to whom I am deeply indebted. They are the cast and script writers of *M*A*S*H*. They walk the human tightrope between tragedy and comedy with so much style and so much caring. They have made me laugh on some of the grimmest days, and for that I owe them all a genuine, heartfelt thank you.

14

I would like to describe the kindnesses of so many others, but I can only mention a few, Kay Carstons, Midge and Ed Clark, Wilma Drysdale, Donna Gilton, Do and Jiggs Johnson, Bruce Jordan, Ann Kinzie, Ed and Cynthia Lasker, Susie and Tom O'Neil, Ad Penberthy, Joel Rothman, Bob Scripps, Ellen and Peter Strauss, Dr. Abraham Halpern, Joy Harris, Peg and Peter Kinney, Kristi Witker, and Robert Stewart, a very kind editor who had to separate the wheat from the chaff, without hurting my feelings. To all of you, and many more, my thanks. You have helped to make me strong.

JEAN HARRIS
January 1986

Introduction

Slowly I came to realize that there was no power capable of changing the image of my person lodged in the supreme court of human destinies, that the image in question (even though it bore no resemblance to me) was much more real than my actual self; that I was its shadow and not the other way round; that I had no right to accuse it of bearing no resemblance to me, because I bore the guilt for the lack of resemblance; that the lack of resemblance was my cross, to bear on my own.

Milan Kundera
The Joke

1.

It is spring as I begin to put the pieces of a book together. Six springs have gone by since Hy died. Until now, I haven't accepted the reality of that. Only the sheer weight of numbers forces me to accept it now—now, when the hurting should be going away, I feel it still. Until today, the only comfort had been not to think about either of us. Anything that touched upon Hy or me was an open wound. But it's time the wound were attended to. That is part of my reason for writing, but only part.

I live today in a top security prison in Bedford Hills, New York, convicted of murdering Dr. Herman Tarnower, Hy as his friends knew him, and sentenced to stay here for fifteen years to life. To live each day with the knowledge that I am responsible for Hy's death, that a man who loved life, and one who appreciated the gift of life more than anyone I have ever known, died because of me is the worst punishment of all. It was my gun. I brought it loaded to Hy's room. To be the instrument of death and to be a murderer are two quite different things. But Hy is no less dead and no one can feel his death as I do. There hasn't been a day I haven't mourned him. There hasn't been a day I haven't missed him. There hasn't been a day I haven't inadvertently called someone else Hy. There hasn't been a day I haven't wished him back.

But wishing is for candles on birthday cakes. Wishing is for children, and children play a role in this book too, an important role. I wish so many things for children and many days those wishes seem almost as hopeless as wishing Hy back on the eighteenth tee at the Country Club, or back on the salmon stream at Runnymede, or back in the office in Scarsdale, being what he loved most to be, a good doctor.

Children are the true parents of this book, my own and the children of women I have come to know during these excruciating six years. Indeed most of the mothers confined here with me in the Bedford Hills Correctional Facility are younger than my own children. I think of them as children too, our children, yours and mine.

Fortunately, I cannot imagine what it must feel like to have your mother, someone who had been the center of your life, someone you loved and were proud of—and affectionately teased and called Big Woman—suddenly turned into a public freak, called by every grim name the media could contrive, from

"Diet Doc Junkie" to "Blue-Blooded Butcher." Overnight I became a cottage industry. Everyone had something to say about me and it was all for sale. *True Detective* magazine carried a lurid twenty-page monstrosity about "The Scarsdale Diet Doc and the Socialite Headmistress." *New York* magazine repeated the same headline, and *Hustler* magazine reduced me to a lewd cartoon, side by side with Charles Manson. *Mad* magazine found the aging mistress and the "Diet Doc" genuine knee-slappers, as did Don Imus on morning radio. Four books were written. I was "the woman scorned," the "power-hungry headmistress," and, finally, as frosting on the cake, "the fornicator." That last touch was added by *Washington* magazine, quoting, of all people, Barbara Keyser, the woman who preceded me as headmistress of Madeira. What follows will hardly be a list of all the things that I am not, but perhaps, for good or for ill, it will help expose the mother of David and Jim Harris as the woman she is. It is late, and little enough to do for them.

Hy fared little better in the press than I did, because the people who knew us least talked the most. He could have shrugged off *Time*'s choice of adjectives about him: "brilliant, austere, humorless, egotistical"—even rather liked them. But he'd have gagged at Samm Sinclair Baker's statement, "He was a perfect gentleman. Why, I never saw him make any passes at the other women when he came here for dinner." How had the mighty fallen that this should be his epitaph. Hy had probably stopped pinching fannies at the age of thirteen. He had also stopped inviting Samm, author of *The Complete Scarsdale Medical Diet Book*, to his home for dinner after the first invitation.

The all-time high in reportorial folly, and there

were hundreds of qualified applicants, came in an article by Sam Rosensohn of the *New York Post*. In the fourth of a series of articles about me, Rosensohn "revealed" to the reading public that Mrs. Harris had stolen the doctor from another woman. He wrote, "Dr. Herman Tarnower, who remained a bachelor to his death, was seeing Zhou Enlai when he met Jean Harris about 14 years ago." And nobody laughed. Zhou Enlai is, of course, the phonetic spelling of Chou En-Lai, former premier of China. Hy did have dinner with him when he went to China in 1973, but they were hardly "going together" when we met in 1966.

As a matter of fact, Hy was between ladies when we met. The last one had grown weary of waiting for a wedding ring and left him to marry someone else. She came back into his life when the marriage didn't work out, but I didn't learn that until the trial. There are many stories that I have learned since his death which I would most happily not have heard. If every man were judged on the basis of his treatment of women alone, history would be a sorry tale indeed. That doesn't make it good or bad, it only makes it true.

It was my mother who asked, "How can you sit by and let others write about you? It's your life. You lived it." One has little or nothing to say about what is written about you, or by whom, but she was right. I suppose somewhere in the back of my mind the intention has always been there. But there is so much to tell now, such a jumble of caring and thinking and experiencing. How do you wrap it all up neatly, the way Miss Andrews taught us, Roman Numeral I, an introduction with a good topic sentence; Roman Numeral II, the body of the story with A's and B's and C's; and Roman Numeral III, the conclusion? What is the topic sentence?

On Friday, March 7, 1980, which was the Friday before I left the Madeira School for good, I had expelled four seniors, who had been caught with marijuana in their rooms. The reasons are long since unimportant, because the Madeira board of directors' first worldly act, after I left, was to tell these students they could come back to graduate. The chairman of the board had told me, "I support your decision completely." One can only forgive, I suppose. It must be very nerve-wracking to be on the board when the headmistress is indicted for murder. If it occurred to any of them that I was innocent they didn't bother to tell me.

There were mixed emotions among the girls about the expulsion. Some stopped by in groups of three or four and said they were sorry, but they supported the decision because it was the right thing to do if we really cared about the school's honor code. Other girls were incensed. One of them called an all-school meeting, read a poignant message, and then screamed "you fucking hypocrites" at the members of the faculty. The academic dean felt I was too hard on the girl when I called her in and laced her out. The dean followed her out of my house, spoke with her for a few minutes and then bounced cheerfully back. "I told her it would have been all right if she had screamed 'you fucking assholes,'" she said. "It was the word 'hypocrite' that made you mad." I have become so accustomed to that kind of language in prison, I tend to forget it was used at Madeira too.

The dean was partially right. The word "hypocrite" was a soul-searing word for me. Had anyone asked during most of my life, "Will the people of integrity please stand up," I would have stood up tall and straight without an instant's hesitation. As a

21

young woman, I was so sure of my values and of what the right answers were. Now I was struggling to be sure. I had given a speech on the subject of integrity the summer before Hy's death at my alma mater, Laurel, a school for girls in Cleveland. The faculty and administration had asked me to give a "keynote address" at the seminar they were having. I spent two months thinking about integrity, and as with so many things, the more I thought about it the more complicated it became.

Here, in part, is what I said:

The hard part today is not how you respond to values so much as deciding what the values will be. While I was growing up values were easy to list. Definitions were simple then, and patterns of behavior were so proscribed that soul-searching about integrity seemed an unnecessary activity. Today we can't even define who is dead, let alone who is behaving well. Sophistry and relativism didn't mar that wonderful, comfortable, platonic approach I grew up with. We were told, and we believed, that there is objective truth, and the highest truth has ethical value. We were told that the pursuit of truth and knowledge is an intrinsically good activity . . .

I think the best definition I have found of integrity is "unflinching adherence to high standards." The unflinching part is key, since you can only imagine a person of integrity constantly assailed from every corner, yet mature, responsible, and courageous enough to hang tough. To some there are rather prim, stern connotations about the word, something that smacks a bit of blue stockings. This is a stereotype we must rid ourselves of if we are going to teach integrity to young people in today's world. Unfortunately—or fortunately, whichever the case may be—the lonely cry in all of us not to be nothing, to make some sign upon the universe is not answered by proprieties. If you at Laurel, and the parents who send their daughters here, truly subscribe to the concept that "the individual is most productive in a climate of freedom of the intellect and of the spirit," we need to think deeply about the implications of that in today's world. A young woman of integrity has high standards, but they are not necessarily your standards or mine, and she is not necessarily your idea of "a good little girl." She is strong, imaginative, courageous, and she can give you a lot of grief.

Hy, in his considerable wisdom, never pondered on a subject as long as I. "God! You're like a dog with a bone," he said sometimes when I wouldn't let go. I read a quotation in *Harper*'s recently that reminded me of Hy: "The powerful know that complexity is the province of underlings." It makes me smile.

I had written my Laurel School lecture as though only the young were struggling for answers. I had made the same mistake Dr. Buffy Miles, Madeira's consultant psychiatrist, made after Hy was dead. "Madeira students," she said, "are still in the process of forming and becoming, so they may be more seriously damaged by the indictment of their headmistress than grown-ups who are not in as vulnerable a stage of life as the girls."

It is a popular myth, but a myth nonetheless. We are "forming and becoming" all of our lives. As adults we are vulnerable too; in fact, the more we know and the more we understand, the more life will touch us. Children enjoy the circus; adults marvel at it. There is never a moment in our lives, in our society at least, when we "grow up." There is nothing simple like a lion to kill, or six months in the Outback to survive, and I say "simple" not disrespectfully but in the sense that these challenges have a specific beginning and ending. If you are a thoughtful person you spend your whole life asking "Why?" and "How?" and "Is this what I wanted?" or "Is this what they meant?"

Of all the myths that I grew up with (they seemed pleasant and safe and agreeable for the most part; in fact, it often saddened me that so many had been shattered and not replaced with equally agreeable ones) the most destructive, the one that left me most vulnerable, was the one that said, "Because you grow older—or when you grow older—you grow up." Not so. You appreciate more, you wonder more at the beauty and sadness of life, and you become familiar with some of the odds so you can avoid—or teach your children to avoid—things that usually turn out badly, like running in front of cars, or playing with matches, or engaging in sex before you know what love is.

But if you are a thoughtful person, and a reasonably brave person, wanting to live life fully, you will always be tempted to touch new kinds of fire, and then have to make peace with the person you were before. Having learned the rules—those absolutes right and wrong—you soon discover that as humans we seldom have the luxury of absolute choice between the two.

After Hy died, a dear friend, Gladys Rusk, wife of Dr. Howard Rusk, wrote me many warm, hopeful, heartfelt letters. She was dying of cancer at the time, one of those long, terrible, painful deaths. But she rarely mentioned herself. After her death Howard sent me some of the notes and quotes and favorite poems that she had collected in a special notebook over the years. Among them was this quotation from John Middleton Murry:

> *For the good man to realize*
> *that it is better to be whole*
> *than to be good*
> *is to enter on a straight and*
> *narrow path compared to which*
> *his previous rectitude was*
> *flowery license.*

More than anything I could put into words, this describes what I believed and what I lived by after I met Hy. Whether it is reason or rationalizing, wisdom of wishful thinking, for me it was true.

I had been proud of my relationship with Herman Tarnower for many years. We were two useful people, stimulating one another, sharing the pleasures of learning new things together, but living quite separate lives too. There had been many women in Hy's life. He was a bachelor, interesting, rich, with an ego that needed attention. He led a merry life, but that was something I carefully closed my eyes to or joked about. When his relationship with another woman began to rub off on my life in ugly, dirty ways, my personal struggle over integrity became increasingly complicated. It was a relationship that had gone on for years, and even when I moved as far away as Virginia it did not come to a halt. Should I walk away without flinching or stay without flinching? And how could I be objective enough to figure out the answer? It was one of many things troubling me deeply that

25

2.

The headline in *The Madeira Spectator*, the school newspaper, read "Dr. Buffy Miles Aids Madeira in Trying Times." The doctor is quoted as saying the girls "would have a hard time understanding the circumstances of the relationship between Mrs. Harris and Dr. Herman Tarnower." As far as I know she didn't question why Mrs. Harris wanted to die. At bottom, the circumstances of the relationship revolved around my need for strength, and my vain efforts to stop being a bleeding heart and be more like Dr. Tarnower.

Hy's strength came from caring first and foremost about himself, doing what he wanted to do, and doing it well. This is not a criticism. Quite the contrary. I believe, without a trace of rancor or cynicism, that the need to like and to love oneself is the first, most positive and productive rule of life. The absence of self-love in the women I live among today is probably their outstanding quality and their first tragedy.

For most of my life "self-love" had a selfish, pejorative ring to it. It wasn't "nice." I spent years looking for my self-esteem in others. But self-love doesn't preclude manners or systems or rules or laws or whatever name we choose to give the parameters within which each society lives. It says "Love yourself first, for good and positive reasons, and then reach out to love others." Don't spend a lifetime expecting to find your identity in mommy or daddy or husband or lover or children. It's an unfair burden to lay upon them, and it's a fool's errand right from the start because your identity can only be found where it is—in you.

People are constantly asking me whether I have changed in prison. Learning is by definition change, and, circumscribed as my life is today, it has opened up avenues of learning and understanding that my former life could never have made possible. I have learned much, about myself, and about others. Much to my surprise, I have learned that I am a survivor, something I never intended or even wanted to be.

The woman who stood by Hy's bed that night, raised a gun to her temple, took a deep breath, and pulled the trigger, is still alive, still functioning. Though there should have been a bullet in that chamber, and wasn't, I don't, as some people tell me, think God was saving me for something special. I think it was, as so much of life is, as Hy's death was, a roll of the dice, something without a plan or a sensible reason, something that shouldn't have been but was.

For several years I thought that Hy had taken most of me with him. For both our sakes I'm happy to discover that it isn't so. Who then is this media creature, this "convicted murderer" who put down the chalk one afternoon, after thirty-six years in a classroom, and walked out to a battery of flashbulbs and headlines and hype? Does anyone care who she is? I finally do, so something useful must have happened in these six impossible years.

But where do all the children who were a big part of the reason for writing this book come in? Where indeed? They are the children of inmates. They fill my life here at Bedford; they motivate me; they make me laugh; they break my heart. They teach me about a world I never knew. They frighten me about its future. I have learned from them, for the first time, how truly underprivileged many of America's children are, and I would like to shout it from the housetops. Children have been the center of my life almost since I stopped being one myself, but not the same children in the same way. The child I was and the children I raised were not average American children, however average and run-of-the-mill we may have seemed to ourselves.

For me there were summer homes and servants, private schools, and a family of six that ate every breakfast and dinner together, lunch too on Saturdays and Sundays and holidays, even if you came in late the night before. Whatever package it may have come in, there was security, total security, a world in which we never doubted that bad things only happened to bad people.

For my own children, the servants were missing, but the rest was there, and I soon learned to double in brass as laundress, plumber, cook, school teacher, as well as wife, mother, and hostess. After my divorce I even bought a round dining-room table so it wouldn't look as though someone were missing. Unfortunately, geometry notwithstanding, no matter where you put the placemats there are four sides to a circle. It took me a while to be convinced, but my children knew it right away.

My lessons here in this large and foreign world began on February 28, 1981, the day I was convicted of "murdering Dr. Herman Tarnower." Since that day those lessons have taken me from the prison kitchen in the medical building, where I scrubbed and cleaned and observed the advanced art of stealing food, to a high school equivalency class where I was called a "Teacher's Aide," to the prison nursery, to a program called South Forty, and finally to the Children's Center where most of my work is presently done. With the opportunity to be with young mothers and children I began to feel alive again, after almost two years of wandering through a deep fog. The more I saw the more I wanted to learn and to share.

With a young friend, another inmate named Dolores Donovan, I began working on a book of children's letters to their mothers in prison. Dolores did most of the collecting, and I did most of the writing—that is, an introduction and a conclusion to tie all the letters together. It would be small, we thought, a simple little book. But nothing that touches human life is simple. By now I should have remembered that. Moreover, letters from children whose mothers are in prison are rarely cute or funny, the kind the public enjoys reading, those nifty little books we use as stocking stuffers.

Even the few pictures they draw are often sad. The subjects are sad and the lack of creative vitality and self-assurance that they reflect are sad as well. Here's a picture of a child crying, "Why did it have to be you, Mama?" The tears are almost as large as the child. Here's a child imagining the day mother will get out. "Free at last, Ma, free at last." Here's a picture of mother, stick figure, no neck, arms protruding from the head, an average drawing for a three-year-old but not for the seven-year-old who drew it.

And here's a cheerful note under a better picture of mother, "You may be twenty-six, Mama, but you still got your looks." Encouragement like that means a lot.

But there were some who found the letters "boring" and "too much alike." I found them heart wrenching. When Dolores was granted clemency, I put them aside. "The public will only sneer at them anyway," I thought. "These letters could never mean to those outside what they mean to me. I *know* these children." One tends to grow egocentric in prison. "Nobody knows the trouble I've seen. Nobody but Jesus."

Happily it is not my nature to indulge in that kind of misery indefinitely. Too many things outside of myself are interesting and important to me, and with age, perhaps even a modicum of wisdom, things that once seemed separate and disconnected have begun to come together in my mind as a living whole. Things I had thought of as the "right thing to do," or "the kind thing to do," or "the intelligent and obvious thing to do" have begun to acquire a broad new relevance. And I realize now that the children's letters are only part of the story to be told.

It would be hard to find a woman who had lived out her life more totally steeped in all the comfortable mythology about America and Americans than I. But observing from a new place, experiencing, listening, searching, reading widely, and questioning have dispelled many of the myths. I finally know how true it is that ignorance is bliss, but only for the ignorant, and not forever, even for them.

The purpose of this book is not to make you cry, and certainly not to romanticize or sentimentalize crime, but to make you care enough to become actively concerned and curious, to unload a few myths of your own, and prepare yourself to make some hard decisions in the years ahead about the role of children in America's future. Is it possible to build a moral society for them based on little more than the constraints of punishment, inflicted quite often by wrongdoers?

If anything that follows sounds like a blow to feminism, that isn't my intent either. To all the ladies who have become president of the bank or a partner in the firm, I say, "Right on! And bully for you!" I also say someone with a good education, the ability to think logically, who knows what it means to have a good parent and be one too, better be having a few babies along the way. And, some feminists notwithstanding, once those babies are born, someone must raise them, someone knowledgeable and caring about the needs of children—which doesn't mean the first warm body you can hire to cuddle them in front of the soaps all day. I wish I knew how to arouse the same concern for children that so many Americans express today for fetuses. While people march on Washington, and throw bombs at Planned Parenthood offices, ostensibly for the unborn, I know of few marches in behalf of prenatal care for mothers or postnatal care for infants. If Simone Weil is correct, and "indignation is the purest form of love," I'm afraid we use up our indignation too early in the life cycle, and children spend the rest of their lives paying the piper. It was not just for the right to life that our much revered Mr. Jefferson thumped the drum. He added "liberty and the pursuit of happiness."

What follows is not, I repeat vehemently, not a feminine whimper from "the belly of the beast." I have not been there, and had I been there I would have little to offer that would serve ordinary people like you and me. This is a voice that once lived in the world you live in, the world which by your daily acts or failures to act, you help to create. What happens here reflects the values of your world. The women you meet here could be you. Their children could be yours.

Part I

Cleveland Heights:
The Early Years

*Human language is a cracked kettle on which
we beat out tunes for bears to dance to, when all
the while we want to move the stars to pity.*
Flaubert

1.

I am a stranger to you, all the more a stranger
because you may have read about me. Notoriety,
painful as it is, is a most effective way to become
anonymous, lost and buried in verbal garbage. It may
give some validity to what follows if I describe to you
as best I can, the person I am, and how I came to see
this piece of the world as I do.

It smacks of relativism, though relativism has a
pejorative ring to it in my ears, to suggest, as I will,
that anyone in prison deserves more than the back of
one's hand. Perhaps I am an echo of my mother and
grandmother who lived out their lives believing that
love conquers all, not romantic love, but love for one's
fellow man.

I don't remember either of them ever saying an
unkind word about another human being. Granted,
they never experienced the no-man's land of prison,
but that doesn't screen one completely from reality.
Most of the wicked never go to prison. Less than 10
percent of reported violent crimes result in incarcera-

35

tions; of that 10 percent, 5 percent of the incarcerated are innocent. Even today with over 500,000 people in prison, and more than ten million in and out of jail during the course of a year, the beat goes on; someone just committed perjury; someone is about to be hurt; someone just rented a woman's body; someone just sold a quantity of drugs, and someone, perhaps an acquaintance or relative of yours, just bought it.

My own first brush with "those less fortunate than we are," our comfortable middle-class euphemism for the poor and the black, came many years ago, and I remember it vividly. I was a junior at Laurel School, a girls' college preparatory school in Cleveland, Ohio, a school like Madeira which the media always mistakenly refers to as a "a finishing school." On Thursday afternoons Laurel juniors climbed into station wagons—they were new then and the sides were wood, not metal painted to look like wood—and drove to a Settlement House to do volunteer work. I had a music and story-telling group, and I went that first day feeling grown-up and secretly suspecting that it was terribly nice of me to be going at all. There was a certain drama about it. I was going to spread happiness all over the place for "those less fortunate than we."

The children in my group at the settlement house were eight to ten years old; there were more than twenty of them. They didn't want to hear a story, and they raised hell all afternoon. I think, looking back to my childhood, I had decided that if you were poor you were lacking something more than money and you owed it to society to compensate for your inadequacy. Many people still think the same way. I told my mother about what had happened, adding, "You'd think poor children could at least be polite." I've remembered her answer all my life, naive perhaps, but laced with deep truth. She said, "You know, Jean, most of these little children have mothers who go out to work, and when they get home they're just too tired to say 'No.'"

It isn't true of all tired working mothers all of the time; I know because I was one for many years, but it's true of some, and it's the beginning of tragedy, of not knowing what the boundaries are, floundering in space. "No," I learned early, can be a loving thing to say. One rarely convinces one's children of it until they begin to say it to their own children. But loving, I have discovered, is something many of the women I live among have had little of, while I, I realize late, have had much, or at least something that was meant to be love.

Indeed there has been much happiness in my life, so much to be grateful for—two fine healthy sons, a deep love, health, laughter, music, interesting work, good books, armfuls of zinnias, and dogs that wagged their tails in greeting when I came home, I wonder how my story could have such a sad ending. If I had to give only one reason I would blame it on physical weakness, the inability to keep slogging along anymore and a genetic whim that has touched more than one member of my family, the same thing that destroyed my father's life and caused an uncle to commit suicide. The psychiatrist would probably start with "your relationship with your father."

The forensic psychologist who tested me for hours after Hy's death said, "I believe from the beginning of your relationship with Dr. Tarnower you experienced what could only be called 'partial death.' You permitted part of yourself to be consumed by the relationship." My husband said once, "You'll never be happy because you don't know what you want." Maybe he was closet to the target, though certainly for a long time I thought all I wanted was to do "the right thing," to be sugar and spice and everything nice with a star in the middle of my forehead, a paragon of someone else's devising.

It never occurred to me that life is something you plan for, with your own list of priorities, not society's. The result, as I look at myself, was an earnest but wimpy character, running all the way, tripping along behind the world, trying to do all the things that were expected, or that I thought were expected, and finally giving up.

I was the last kid on the block to stop believing in Santa Claus; I cried when my doll was broken; I cried when my feelings were hurt; I was at college before I cared enough or dared enough to figure out what a virgin is. My trousseau was picked out by my mother, with a hat to match every dress. And I still have no sense of direction, so when the man at the gas station says, "Turn left, three more blocks and it's on your left, you can't miss it," I always miss it. I either know exactly where I am or I'm hopelessly lost, or I feel hopelessly lost. There were many times when Hy didn't know how to get where we were going, but he was always relaxed about it. If it isn't this street it's probably the next one. I always wanted to stop and ask.

As I think about it, the getting lost thing is important. When I made a wrong turn it wasn't annoyance I felt, it was sheer, stark terror. I once called Hy in tears from a gas station in White Plains and asked him to come and lead me home. I was sure from where I was that I was going to wind up on the Bronx River Parkway. Hy was kind, arrived shaking his head, and led me home.

Over the years when I was silly enough to say which way I thought we should turn, he would pat me

38

on the knee, shake his head and say, "Well, there's one thing be said for you, Jean. You're consistent. You're always wrong."

I don't try to be wrong, but it's been a long time since I was afraid to be. I made my way through most of my life like the man who broke the bank at Monte Carlo, with an independent air, but always aching for someone to hold me and assure me, "everything's going to be all right."

From the time I was a little girl I was told in a hundred different ways that there was "right" and there was "wrong" and "good" people do "the right thing" and "bad" people do "the wrong thing." It made sense, and it's a great timesaver. Any decision making was lifted from my hands leaving me ample time to do the things I enjoyed doing, like reading and writing, singing, swimming, and playing with the dog.

Hy played a key role in uninhibiting me, and he was not forever after glad. I stopped presuming to tell the world what the rules should be, but having discovered what they were, I didn't pretend it wasn't so. Hy, like most of his friends, was perfectly comfortable with immorality as long as nobody mentioned it, and everybody was nicely dressed. I always called a whore a whore. It isn't an endearing quality.

Feelings were something never discussed as I was growing up. The subject was treated a little like where babies come from. They were just something you kept to yourself. Hy preferred it that way too. My feelings were vented on the beach in Canada, where I spent my first forty summers, and later along the ocean in Palm Beach. I breathed them out to the wind and the waves and the hot summer sun. I swung my arms wide and breathed deep, and dove into the water and swam out far and swam for hours without a qualm or a fear.

The closest thing to the facts of life I learned in my parent's home was the message on a picture that hung down in the "recreation room." It was a picture of an old man and underneath it read, "My only regrets are the temptations I have successfully resisted." I thought it was funny and rather wicked, but I didn't know exactly why. Temptation, as any fool knew, was something "good people" didn't yield to, so he must be bad, and bad was sort of funny.

I was eighteen before I heard the word "divorce," at least heard it in a way I remember. Mother called my older sister and me into the library and told us in hushed tones that Mr. and Mrs. X, old family friends, were getting a divorce. Mr. X had met "a woman from Chicago." None of the scarlet ladies of history past or present could have aroused in my imagination a more despicable creature than "the woman from Chicago." I never even felt quite the same about Chicago again.

I pictured Mr. X eating solitary lunches at the University Club for the rest of his life. Certainly "nice" people would never have anything to do with him again. But of course they soon did. And Mrs. X? She started teaching school, and after her friends had all taken her to the movies a few times she went about the business of growing old—alone. But everyone always admired her tremendously.

The things you've been told often have little to do with the things you observe and experience. A healthy distrust of idealism is much to be desired and admired, but I didn't have it. I'm not sure you can always recognize the difference between high standards and flaccid, sentimental idealism, even in yourself, even when you're trying to recognize it. Sincerity itself is a much overrated virtue.

I was constantly telling someone that any good idea carried to its logical conclusion becomes an absurdity, but I didn't spend much time applying that statement to morality. It too, pushed past a certain point, can become moral fanaticism and quite incompatible with individual freedom and diversity. I think of myself as a very logical person, but a literal person, too, though the two are often mutually exclusive. I need clarity and definite answers. Hy relished detachment and ambiguity. He was quite comfortable in the moral penumbra that had settled over our world. I have talked glibly for years about how the young must be taught to be comfortable with life's ambiguities, but the truth is I have never been very comfortable with many of them myself.

For the first forty-two years of my life I boxed myself into a world of moral absolutes, and like Santayana's *Last Puritan* I hardly got so far as to feel at home in this absurd world. I was slow to realize that reason and goodness are sometimes secondary and incidental.

My "absolutist conscience" remained for years, "a pretender, asserting in exile its divine right to the crown." "You can't tell Jean anything. She thinks she knows everything" was a familiar refrain as I grew up. My mother called me "Miss Infallible" when I was being too self-righteous to bear. When self-righteousness spilled over into overt rudeness she washed my mouth out with Lifebuoy, or even worse, wouldn't let me play with my doll house.

I never pinpointed anything I wanted of life until I had two sons, and wanted zealously for them to have healthy minds and bodies, and the strength and self-confidence I feigned but lacked; and then when I had met Hy to know he would always be there, to love and to run to, however far the run might be. All my life

41

my prayer for each day was the same, "Watch over the family, and give me the strength to do what I must, and get through the day."

Freud said, "The unanswerable riddle of the ages is 'What does a woman want?'" Maggie Scarf in her book *Unfinished Business* asked, "What do women at various stages of their lives require in order to live?" I don't know the answer for others, but I suspect it is primarily a feeling of security, a knowing that somewhere reachable there is safe ground where for a little while at least the hurting stops, someone touches you or talks to you, or really listens to you, and the hurting stops. When that place is too far away, and one seldom gets there, and the pounding never lets up, sometimes a person gives up. One's inward life and outward life come together in an ill-timed, indigestible stew and throwing it all up isn't insanity, it's the only thing the brain and the body can do.

The brutal truth of this I found out on a Monday afternoon, March 10, 1980, sometime after 3:00 P.M. I left my office where I had served for three years as headmistress of the Madeira School, stopped at my secretary's office to say, "I'm leaving, Carol. I've had enough," and went home to write my will, a few personal notes, and gather together insurance papers that the boys would need. It was the culmination of ten years of a growing depression.

Whether it was a lifetime of feeling inadequate, or the mysterious chemistry of my brain that had led me to that point, I do not know for certain, but I will always believe it was the latter, an explosion of anguish over which I no longer had control, which I only knew had to end.

I hate the knowledge that I gave up, but given the same combination of pressures and traumas and

42

hurts, I might do it again. Only might. I'm stronger now. And ten years of prescribed drugs about which I knew nothing, and Hy knew too little, are behind me as well. It wasn't fear of hard work or seven-day work weeks that did me in. The one true blessing until that day had been to be perpetually busy.

Yet in all the soul-searing, soul-searching months and years since Hy's death the one regret I have not felt is walking away from Madeira, and from a job that many people, both men and women, aspire to. I see that glorious view of the Potomac River stretched out as my front yard, and for me it is a picture of loneliness and impotence too deep to explore. It wasn't cowardice or self-pity or ineptness or jealousy that brought me down. It was simple unvarnished exhaustion from caring too much and trying too hard, and feeling utterly alone in the process. Intellectually I believe I know some of the answers to life's problems, but I couldn't seem to apply them to my own life anymore. I was a good teacher and an ineffectual self.

Perhaps it went way back to my growing up a priggish little girl and woman to the onlooker, but filled to the bottom of my soul with that immortal longing to love and be loved. If any character of the Bible had left his indelible mark on me it was wise old Noah. Two by two he welcomed them to the ark, and I don't think for a moment he'd have wasted time building it for any other reason. We are all needed by each other, without sharing there is only emptiness. I am not totally unrealistic. I know perfectly well that sooner or later someone has to empty the garbage and pay the grocer, but I'm still tempted, given the choice, to take one daffodil for ten shares of IBM.

Whatever it was that my father did to mold me into the kind of woman I became, I'm not sure; but most of the molding was done by default, never by sitting down and talking or sharing ideas. He was a difficult man. He was more than a difficult man. I'm afraid, he was a tortured man. His inner doubts came out in striving all his life to be very good at what he did, which he was—but in a deep, cancerous bitterness as well.

He really didn't like anyone. He died shortly after Hy did. I think the tragedy and turmoil of Hy's death hastened the death of both my parents. Dad's was a quiet and peaceful death and for that all of his children were grateful. It was a kind of death one would wish for all of us. Perhaps for him it was only fair. His life was not peaceful, and I do not believe it was happy. He avoided happiness almost as one would avoid a situation he knew he couldn't handle.

The only thing he really loved was his work. I grew up believing that nothing in the world was more important than "what Daddy did." He designed steel plants and oil refineries, some of the largest all over the world, from Magnitogorsk in the Urals to Brasília in the jungles of Brazil, from the panhandle of Texas to Oil City, Pennsylvania, from Trinidad to India and back. I loved hearing him talk about all the places he had been.

My summer in Russia several years before I met Hy was prompted by the bits and snatches of information about that great enigma that I had heard from my father. But it wasn't easy to get him to talk about anything but the job itself, Aramco, Bechtel, Standard Oil, Petróleo Mexicano—these were what peopled his world—not people themselves. I didn't understand all the reasons "Daddy" traveled so much, or what he did "at the office," but whatever it was I never questioned that it helped keep the world's wheels turning.

It was so important that no one, not even my mother, was ever permitted to call him at the office. It was all just too important ever to be interrupted. I remember the first time I called Hy at the clinic, hesitantly and apologetically, and was amazed that he didn't sound angry, or too busy to talk.

My father's professional life was colorful and successful. His home life was not. He seemed to need what I still feel was an inordinate amount of praise and thanks. I don't think I visited him for thirty-five years that I didn't some time early in the visit find myself thanking him for sending me to college. There was never a moment when he seemed to realize that his children were now doing all those same things— even paying taxes, something he never stopped believing was a very personal affront that Congress had meted out to him.

I don't remember my father ever hugging me, or holding me on his lap—or hugging any of us. I don't remember a special joke, or his saying something funny or silly. I know he loved Christmas and he wanted it to be special and wonderful for us. He was very generous, but somehow before the tree was up and it was time to enjoy, his temper over the lights, and where the pliers were, had frightened too much of the joy away. His anger terrified me. I can remember running to my room and wrapping a blue satin comforter over my head to drown out the sounds of it. Like Hy he was a bright, talented man. Unlike Hy he rarely took the time to enjoy. I don't remember his ever exclaiming over a full moon, or a beautiful fall day, or an armful of flowers.

From the time I was a little girl I was forever bringing flowers into the house, starting, I suppose, with dandelions and burdocks. Years later the first graders in my classes always loved Edna St. Vincent Millay's poem that ends "She said, 'Oh what a fine bouquet,' but later on I heard her say 'She's always bringing in those weeds.' " By the time I could drive at the cottage up in Canada I knew for twenty miles around where the fields of wild sweet pea or black-eyed Susan or tiger lilies or Queen Anne's lace and thistle were.

And all the farmer's wives would sow a row or two of zinnias and asters and calendulas in with the beets and carrots and lettuce. At least once a week I would gather buckets of flowers and then spend a happy part of a day arranging them. My son David now has the handsome blue mixing bowl that always spent August in the middle of the long dining-room table ablaze with every color of zinnia. How I wish my father might have enjoyed at least one such simple pleasure.

Hy found the same pleasure in trees that I found in flowers. I loved walking with him any time of the day, any time of the year while he exclaimed over a cut leaf maple, or worried about the way the three birches near the pond looked, and especially when he just breathed deeply and said, "God! Aren't we lucky." It was balm for all of life's wounds—whatever had hurt or ached ceased to exist. And sometimes when we stood there on a rainy day or a moonlit night or a cold, snowy morning and he put his arms around me I felt as though the whole world could fall down on me and I would walk away unscathed. I knew moments of peace and happiness and a blessed feeling of "safeness" with Hy that were beyond anything I could have read about or imagined.

When Dad was traveling, which was most of the time, I remember my childhood as peaceful and pleasant. The moments that come most quickly to mind are moments spent alone, lying on a large blue sofa with my feet up over the back of it, looking out the window at a huge flowering almond tree; walking along the road that led to the cottage, the elm tree that grew beside the gate, and a picture-book maple tree that grew in the wheat field just to the right of our gateway. It was too beautiful to cut down so Mr. Hill plowed and planted around it for years, until it was struck by lightning. I never stopped missing it after it was gone. The field always seemed eerie and empty.

Playing with my doll house was a favorite activity, rearranging furniture, giving names and personalities to the family of dolls that lived there, and often just lying on my stomach, peeking through the curtains at the dolls and the coziness of the house where they lived.

I enjoyed all kinds of make-believe—playing "school" and "office" were favorites. I can still see my dolls propped up on small chairs while I taught them the alphabet, or read them a story. To my parent's despair I was constantly retrieving old bills, and important-looking papers from the waste basket, carrying them around in an old pocket-book of my mother's, or sitting at my desk and making marks on them with red pencil. I remember a stack of old ledgers that my grandfather gave me as one of the great gifts of my life. They were from the little tobacco business that he owned and ran in Baltimore. I played with them all the way home to Cleveland in the back of the car and stashed them in drawers all over the house. My mother called them "trash" and I said they were "important," so Jean's "important trash" became a familiar name and a familiar nuisance to the whole family. I think it took mother about three years, disposing of them a few sheets at a time, to get rid of the whole collection. But by then I was taking dancing lessons and singing lessons and piano lessons so it didn't matter. Mother loved music and theater as much as I did.

It was my mother that I telephoned for the first two years that I was in prison. I was permitted two five-minute telephone calls per month, scheduled at the convenience of the prison, not the prisoner. A guard dialed the number, and when Mother answered, a kitchen timer was set at five minutes. When the bell went off the conversation ended abruptly. The first of three shrieking, screaming, howling scenes that I have given way to in prison was over one of those calls. The C.O. (Correction Officer) found my mother's name, Mrs. Struven, too inconvenient to learn how to pronounce. He called her by her given name, "Mildred."

"This is Jean calling Mildred." It was bad enough to have this unsavory little man call me "Jean" when by directive he is required to call me by my last name, but to have him call Mother "Mildred" was like a knife in the heart. I howled with pain and trembled for hours afterward. It proved to be, of course, an open invitation to most of the C.O.s in the phone room thereafter to call Mother "Mildred" as disrespectfully as they dared.

Deliberate unkindness is something totally foreign to my nature. I am never prepared for it. It always shocks me, it always hurts me, and I usually respond to it in a way that makes the perpetrator want to do it over again. "You're just as big as the things that make you angry, Jean," was one of my mother's favorite remonstrances to me whenever she thought I was overreacting. I'm sure she'd have said the same thing if she had known about the telephone scene. It seemed a very large thing to me at the time.

Our conversations, Mother's and mine, were about everything except where I was: music, the theater, old friends, how the boys were. She always asked how I was and said I sounded fine, but she never once mentioned the word "prison." Her modus vivendi and mine were the same. We simply did not discuss what was unspeakable. It may not be wise but it's one way to survive. I would have sworn I was the last person in the family who would have done anything to hurt her, and I was the one who ended up hurting her the most. I asked her once if she intended to watch a much publicized television program about "the trial." She answered, "Why would I, dear? It has absolutely nothing to do with you."

By the time my father died they had been married for sixty-two years. How much of the woman she had been was left I'm not quite sure. There were sparks of the old humor, and always the love of music. The last time we spoke was on the hundredth anniversary of the Metropolitan, and we shared our pleasure over the televising of the celebration. Two days later, she died in her sleep. The last thing my sister heard her say was, "I've just had a nice talk with Dad." I didn't ask to go to her funeral. A prisoner goes to her mother's funeral in handcuffs and chains, with an armed guard beside her. I had brought her enough sadness. I would never have added more.

Because of the nature of some of my reading, and because I am the daughter of Mildred Witte Struven, I have thought a good deal about religion—thought about it more than I practiced it. I am a thoughtful person, but whether or not I am in any true sense a religious person I cannot say. I am forever taking the Lord's name in vain which is a poor beginning, and it was also a source of sorrow to my deeply religious mother. She, when pushed almost beyond human endurance, would say "doggone it" and then look a little embarrassed by her outburst. I think of Hy and my mother as archetypical survivors, one with an abiding faith and one with an abiding ego. Take your pick. Trying to think your way down the .middle is idiot's delight.

I was brought up in the Episcopal church, but then where else for the "socialite headmistress of the exclusive Madeira School"? My sons were both confirmed in the Episcopal church, and we all attended church together regularly for years. I began to be a little disillusioned with the whole thing when I needed help and felt the church had turned its back, too consumed with its social life.

But maybe that isn't fair. Rewriting the service in the vernacular spoiled the lovely old familiarity, the feeling of "going home" I once had on Sunday mornings. Before Hy's death I went to church occasionally, but by then I never knew what page we were on. Considering what society was doing to all the other familiar things I had once found comforting and supportive, I think the church might have left the communion service alone for a little while longer—at least until the class of '45 "passed on."

I believe in God and in the very deep-seated human need for ritual, for doing a certain thing in a certain way repeatedly—not to make God happy but to make humans feel safe. You shouldn't have to decide about everything all the time. Although he was an atheist, H. L. Mencken's definition of religion in his *Treatise on the Gods* was one I found reasonable and understandable for years. I haven't the book with me but in essence he said, "Whether it's the hocus-pocus of a dancing Hottentot or the high incantations of a Catholic archbishop, religion is every man's effort to discover the power that controls his destiny, and to persuade that power to be kind." I think there's still a great deal of truth in that.

I realize, as I put myself through the agonizing paces of trying to look at myself objectively, that I am an unfortunate combination of my parents' two most sensitive qualities: my father's volatile drive to over-achieve, and my mother's infinite capacity to love and forgive. It's a self-flagellating combination. And yet I will always think of my life as essentially happy.

I don't even remember adolescence as a painful time, though over the years I've certainly read enough books assuring me it is supposed to be painful. Perhaps that is because I was more adolescent at forty than at fourteen. I have always loved reading, responded with pleasure and excitement to new ideas, and enjoyed the peace and quiet of being alone. That triumvirate of traits removed a great deal of the pain of growing up, but it also slowed down the process.

I can still remember with great clarity some of the significant steps in my learning, and I can see now how each played a small role in developing the attitude that permeates my responses here at Bedford.

Mother was, as mothers are, my first teacher and her familiar homilies have stuck through a lifetime. "Judge people from the neck up, Jean"—that was an early admonition. It disturbed her that I had as a little girl been beguiled by curtsies and felt put out because she didn't require me to curtsy as my friends' mothers did.

"Look people in the eye and say 'How do you do.' A cursty tells you nothing. Judge people from the neck up, Jean." I may have learned the lesson too well. One can be beguiled by talk as well as by curtsies.

I must have been about 2½ years old when my sister, Mary Margaret, read to me my first favorite story. It was about the old woman whose pig wouldn't jump over the stile, so she couldn't get home that night. Fire wouldn't burn stick, stick wouldn't beat dog, dog wouldn't bite pig, and the pig wouldn't jump over the stile. The logic of all that cause and effect was somehow very satisfying and orderly to my mind. Moreover you could make up endless variations of it on your own. I never tired of it.

2.

I don't remember learning to read, though for me it was much like being born. My first big remembered learning plateau was reached in second grade. I wrote some spelling words on the side of a painted green table, and my teacher saw it. It was my introduction to the word "cheating," and it was my first awareness that spelling was something difficult for me. I didn't know at the time that spelling would dog me all my life. I live with a dictionary on my lap and still send out letters that would horrify some of the good English teachers I have had. I don't know whether I'm forgetful or dyslexic. It doesn't much matter now. The results are the same.

In the third grade I helped to build a papier-mâché castle, complete with moat and turrets and draw-bridge and portcullis. Miss Vincent was the lady who let us build it, and I thought of her often when my own classroom was awash with fingerpaints and torn strips of paper and pans full of paste made from flour and water. The castle, which I remember as a splendid castle, taught me there is a thing called history and that history is about people and how they live. It made history a tangible reality.

I cheated again during a fifth grade English test when the question was "What is Deuteronomy?" I copied from somebody else, but she didn't know the right answer either. "Two heads," I have often assured students when I saw them copying, "are not always better than one." After the fifth grade I made my own mistakes. The first question on the history college board I took in 1940 was "How was Delcassé the nemesis for Bismarck?" I had never heard of Delcassé and I didn't know what nemesis meant. Fortunately, it was before Smith was hard to get into.

I haven't been afraid to say, "I don't know" ever since, as student or teacher. I don't enjoy saying it, though, and many of the times that I have had to are still fresh in my memory. Knowing right answers was my security blanket as a student. When I didn't know them I stood naked. Later, when I was the only woman in the room who wasn't married, when I went places because I was "the headmistress" or "Dr. Tarnower's girl" not because I was me, clothes became my security blanket. Whatever they all thought, at least I looked as good as they did.

In seventh grade I learned the word ethnic and made an ethnographic map of the city of Cleveland. I was struck by the fact that when Hungarians came to Cleveland they settled where other Hungarians lived, and Chinese sought out other Chinese, and so with Italians and Swedes and all the others. Up to that time I had belonged to the Great American Melting Pot School, but something about those pinks and greens and blues made it very clear to me that people reach out for what is familiar, what makes them feel safe. People need people who understand them and share their values. The melting pot myth was one of my first to bite the dust. Millions of Americans still

53

believe in it, which is one of the reasons, I suppose, that running for political office in America is such a chancy, difficult, frustrating thing.

Mr. Purvis was my civics teacher that year. I must have liked him very much because he was the only teacher I ever asked to "please write in my pink autograph book." He wrote, "To the spirit of the Phoenix with great good wishes." I had to look up what the Phoenix was and I have absolutely no idea why he wrote it. Perhaps even then the round-bottomed doll that you beat on, but it always bounces back, was taking shape.

I learned to write a proper research paper at Laurel School: outlining, footnoting, bibliographies, all the useful proper stuff. The first substantial independent research paper I wrote was in my senior year at Laurel and was on the Federalist Papers. I had the good fortune to go to Washington that spring, and was allowed to walk into the Rare Books Room in the Library of Congress, without fanfare or special privilege, and hold in my hands, and read from Hamilton's and Madison's and Jay's own copies of the papers, complete with their notes jotted in the margins. The experience was another leg up for my sense of the reality of history, and my personal understanding that the men pictured in Muzzey (our history text) had actually touched my life. It was 1940, and on that same trip we sat in the Senate one night late and watched the Lend-Lease Bill be passed.

I went to Smith College because I heard that Smith didn't have sororities. I knew little or nothing about sororities, but I imagined them as something that would make me extremely uncomfortable. They invoked my two least favorite words: "boyfriend" and "girlfriend." (That was before I fell over "mistress" and "lover.") I have never been much of a joiner, and I pick friends slowly, not in packs, and not because they knew the secret handshake. I couldn't picture myself standing around in a dark room, wearing a long robe, carrying a candle and swearing to do or die for Beta Theta Pi. It wasn't snobbery. It was simply a matter of knowing my own limitations.

My years at Smith were not what one would call "normal." Pearl Harbor was bombed that first December, and the war in Europe ended just before the class of '45 graduated four years later. "The bomb" was still to be dropped. When I read about the war now, years later as an adult, not in *The New York Times* as it happened, it shocks me to think how little it touched me, how appallingly unaware I was of the enormity of what was happening. I have often reminded myself of that when I found the self-absorption of the young particularly galling. For the most part, I dug into an unused storage room in the basement of the Smith library and read for four years.

"Prudish" would probably be a kind description of what I was at Smith, still afraid to take a very honest look at life, still not tempted by the secrets on the other side of childhood. My senior year I took a seminar on international cartels with Mr. Orton, a delightful, tweedy, pipe-smoking Englishman who had been a member of the British Labour Party. There were five of us in the course, and we met at Mr. Orton's house, not far from campus.

The girls stopped one day on the way there to buy a bottle of wine, a daring act in those days. Mr. Orton brought out wine glasses and started to pour. I stopped him at my glass with, "Oh, no thank you. I don't drink." He smiled pleasantly and said, "Well far be it from me, my dear, to lead you down the primrose path," and poured a little extra wine into his own glass. It was one of those uncomfortable moments when I finally realized I was out of place and rather silly.

Mr. Orton has another special place in my memory. The last lecture he gave in one of his courses began like this: "Well I hope by now you are all thoroughly confused." I suppose others may know instinctively that the first step in real learning is figuring out what the questions are. The answers come much later, and perhaps never. But hearing it said out loud made a difference to me. His whole lecture that day seemed wonderfully relevant to me. I sat there listening and enjoying, and trying to write down every word. I still have the notes.

My major was economics, which happily was still a philosophy course in those days. A young man named Keynes was just beginning to be heard from, and a philosophy was about to be renamed or at least finally taken seriously as a science. I think today there are many who might suggest putting it back into the philosophy department. The two college courses that have meant most to me over the years, enriched my life by making me far more aware of the world around me, had nothing to do with economics. One was geology, the other was the history of art. Marshall Schalk, the young instructor of geology who taught me, has been professor emeritus for twelve years now, and writes occasionally to tell me about his grandchildren, and to wish me well. It pleases me that he remembers me. Over the years I have encouraged hundreds of young people to take at least one course in geology and one in art history.

I may have learned a little more about how to think at Smith. A remarkable woman named Esther Cloudman Dunn certainly did her best to make me think, and so did Mr. Orton, and Esther Lowenthal, and others. But I don't remember having much courage in that area until years later. My teachers, right back to the first grade, would say I always thought for myself, but it wasn't so.

I asked a lot of questions, but for all practical purposes, I was monolithically establishment for more than forty years, sure that if the textbook said it, or *The New York Times* said it, or the teacher or the bishop or the Junior League said it, it must be the straight stuff. I clung tenaciously to safe "right" answers. Probably for that reason I graduated Phi Beta Kappa and magna cum laude. The satisfaction that being elected a Phi Beta gave me was contained in the few minutes it took me to race back to my dormitory to call and tell my father before he left for the office.

Twenty years later when I earned my master's degree I could no longer avoid the fact that my thoughts were as valid as the teacher's, even if they weren't the same, even if they were wrong. When I finished an M.Ed. I thought seriously of earning a Ph.D. in philosophy. I wrote a long, earnest paper for my philosophy professor and handed it in feeling that it was very wise and very significant. The professor gave me a B— on it, and his only comment was, "You're a hopeless idealist." The Ph.D. was forgotten. Later I told Hy, "I've earned my doctorate in you." Since his death, I have learned to my sorrow, that I was no better versed in Hy than in philosophy. Another B—.

Grosse Pointe:
Mrs. Harris

I was married in 1946, the year after I graduated from college. I fell into wifehood, and motherhood, and Junior Leaguehood because that's what girls did, not because I thought it through, listed the options, and made a choice. That's not to say I think it's a poor choice. Quite the contrary. I often said to the girls at school, when we were talking about their wonderful plans for the future, "Remember, the best thing there is is a happy marriage." A senior said to me one day, "I can't believe you said that, Mrs. Harris. I really can't believe you would say anything that dumb." A freshman whose mother had been married five times said, "God! If I thought that I wouldn't want to go on living." I was always delighted to find some happy traditionalists in the group who looked forward to marriage and motherhood. Indeed, they are almost the new breed of nonconformists.

I was married to James Scholes Harris and divorced nineteen years later. He was a very nice man. But then this is almost a very nice story. I had known Jim since I was seven years old and he was ten. His family owned a summer cottage near ours in Canada. He was born and brought up in Grosse Point, Michigan, the son of Albert and Helen Harris. His mother was a handsome woman, and a very decent scout, though her first question about anyone was invariably, "Who was her mother?" and out would come the Social Register. My own mother's approach was, "I don't care who she is, I expect her to behave."

In spite of obvious differences in their list of priorities, our mothers got along very well. Our fathers were something else. Mr. Harris—everyone called him "Butts"—was a great favorite of mine from the time I was a little girl. He was short and funny and had a most congenial smile. If he ever got terribly angry, it wasn't when I was around. Even the day Jim threw a firecracker and it exploded on the canvas top of his father's new convertible, he showed great restraint. On weekends he used to sit with me out on the cliff overlooking the lake and watch the cranes fly by.

He had a wonderful library of hundreds and hundreds of books, and he had read them all. I can see him now in the middle of a conversation about almost anything, get up, take down a particular book, flip through it a minute, chuckle and say triumphantly, "Here! Read this. Read this, you'll love it." And I always did. H. L. Mencken was a particular favorite of his and mine—in spite of the things he said about Roosevelt—but then so were Conrad, and William James, and Trollope, and dozens more. He didn't make you analyze them, he just used them to make the subject of the moment mean more. I was given most of his books when he died, and I have packed and unpacked and carried them about for years, reading them, treasuring them, but finally having to give most of them away for want of space.

My fondness for Butts made him a particular target of my father's criticisms, but his unforgivable sin was political. Butts voted for Roosevelt four times! His devotion to Roosevelt was deep. The Harrises lived for years on a little lane called Roosevelt Place. In 1936 the staunch Republicans on the block tried to have the name changed to Theodore Roosevelt Place. Butts fought them and won, but old friendships were strained beyond repair in the process. I'm not sure it was worth the price, but I admired the man very much. He was kind to me and I wish he had lived long enough for my sons to know him. He would have filled a very large void in their lives.

Jim, like his father, was an attractive man, more easy-going, not intellectual. I can't think of any enemies he ever had. He had a kind word for just about everyone, and usually took the time to say it. He went to the University of Michigan, became a Deke, drank beer and schlepped around until the university and his father agreed that the navy was a better place for him.

The Second World War had just begun. He ended up as a lieutenant in the Naval Air Corps and spent several years in places like Ottumwa, Iowa, and several years in places like Green Island, in the South Pacific. He was a navigator on a PBY, picked up pilots out of the ocean, and won the Bronze Star and the Navy Cross. Like many men of his generation he remembered the war years with nostalgia and real affection.

We were married in May 1946 and divorced in 1965. He was a good husband by lots of standards and definitions: no heavy drinking, no extra-curricular women; he cut the grass every weekend and edged the garden, and played baseball with the boys, and thoughtfully asked, "Where do you want to go to dinner?" On weekends we played bridge with old friends, or went to a country club dance. In the summer we chartered a boat with friends, and sailed up into Georgian Bay, or had friends visit us at the cottage in Canada which my father had given us. In winter we took the boys skiing from the time they could barely walk, and usually stayed with friends in an old schoolhouse they had converted to a ski chalet.

What sense does it make to divorce a nice man and a nice life like that? I don't think even he knew the answer and I could never quite explain it myself. When the divorce was final he had said, "All right. You've gotten that out of your system, now let's grow up and get married."

That I write little of Jim does not in any sense diminish him as a very decent man, or reduce him to an irrelevancy. Given his choice were he alive to be asked I'm sure he would say, "Include me out." He wanted to be a good father, and I know his sons remember him with true affection. I find it hard sometimes to remember him. Our life together was a period of marking time, of doing what nice young couples do—or did.

The two things I can remember arguing about with him he was right about, though I certainly didn't think so at the time. He read the newspaper with a proper amount of worldly wariness. I was sure it must be so "because the paper said so." And I was always so smugly positive when I thought I was right. He said people ultimately acted out of self-interest; they did what they did because they wanted to. Not so, said I. Many people acted as they did "for a higher reason. What about the mother who plunges into the sea to save her drowning child?" I asked, sure that the example settled the question. "She does it because she loves the baby and wants it safe—not for the baby

61

but for herself," he answered.

I thought most of us were "nobler" than that. Why I thought it I don't know. It was the accepted mythology of the day, I guess. It sounded so "un-nice" to do something just because you wanted to do it. I didn't leave Jim because he did something "wrong," or I did something "wrong." I wasn't suddenly seized with a burning desire to kick over the traces, do something wild and irresponsible. I simply needed to fill the void that I was finally aware my life consisted of. And it didn't even occur to me that not loving was part of the void.

Years ago *Life* magazine had an article on different kinds of music, and how musical tastes reflected whether you were "upper class, upper middle class, lower middle class, or lower class." My favorites, the golden oldies, were "lower middle class" right across the board. I was in good company though. Cole Porter, Rodgers and Hart, and Noel Coward were there too. Music speaks to me in special ways. The way the aroma of a bakery or a special garden can evoke a whole part of someone's life in one delicious deep breath, a song can bring back moments in my life or express something I can't say in any other way. There were songs, lower middle-class songs if you will, that said to me there is more to life than this.

I used to try to get Jim to talk about the future—some of the things we'd do together, as a family or later when the boys were grown up and on their own. The furthest ahead he ever got was "when the boys get ready for college we can remortgage the house." "Is that all there is? Is that all there is—if that's all there is my friend then let's keep dancing." Right now, right this minute what is an ordinary person like me doing on the other side of the world? What is she thinking, what makes her happy, will she have to gather twigs to make the fire for dinner? Will the parameters of my world always be Jefferson and Lake Shore and Mack Avenue?

I remember one night after we'd been out for the evening, Jim was asleep and I put on my coat, a good black one with a pretty mink collar that is still tacked on a suit or something. I went out to the boys' play yard and swung on a swing and then stretched out on the sand and looked up at the sky and felt a kind of inexpressible longing and frustration. It consumed me. I was part of the sand and part of the trees and part of the earth and I felt not yet born, but maybe, just maybe about to be.

A few nights later the boys were in bed, I had tucked them in and done all the right stuff, I thought, and now my schoolwork was spread on the living room floor and I was planning lessons for tomorrow. But Jimmy kept turning his light on and not going to sleep and Jim went up and put him back to bed and on the way checked the toothbrushes in the boys' bathroom, a favorite activity of his. They were bone dry. I hadn't seen them perform the rites of the toothbrush.

Jim was very cross, and suddenly as he stood there in the living room reviewing my misdemeanors and oversights, I knew it was the end of the marriage. There wasn't an ugly scene or even much of an argument. I simply said, "Jim, it's 10:30 and starting right now I'm not your wife anymore." It was all very civilized and painless for me, not for David and Jim. When they were finally told, they couldn't understand what it meant. They had liked our way of life the way it was.

It all smacked of Dick and Jane. If the house on Hillcrest had had a white picket fence around it, and the Kerry Blue Terrier named Bonnie had been a

63

brown-and-white thing named Spot, you could package it and sell it to Scott Foresman.

It had never occurred to me that I would become a "working woman." My job-hunting was prompted in large part, I think, by my fear of women. I enjoy housecleaning, fussing to make the guest room look pretty, and arranging flowers and such. I do not enjoy women's card parties and luncheons. I am afraid of women. I have spent my entire life, whenever I found myself in a roomful of them, feeling totally out of it, suspecting everybody there knows something I don't know. Secrets! I haven't a single recipe anyone would want; I hated having another woman come into my kitchen, and I was devoutly grateful that they didn't come into the bedroom.

Cute names are my nemesis—Pinky, Punkey, Petey, Suki, Ceci, Kiki—my life has been punctuated by them, each with a tennis racquet slung casually over the shoulder, and a needlepoint cover that zips into place and matches the rick-rack on the tennis dress. A group like that can intimidate the hell out of me, even if I'm thinner, or soberer, or even ostensibly in charge.

Job hunting was a convenient escape hatch. And the closest thing to where I lived that hired women was a private school. It isn't an inspiring beginning to what was to become a happy and successful lifetime career as a teacher, but that's the way it began.

Teaching wasn't the last thing I wanted to do, but if I had ever made a list it would probably have come somewhere near the end. My interest in it grew in spurts as bit by bit I discovered ways to share my own pleasure in learning, and as I discovered the books of great educators. Alfred North Whitehead was a name

I had never heard when I found a copy of his *Aims of Education* with nothing more to speak for it than that it was lying on a table of old paperbacks and marked 10¢. I read it. I devoured it, and was never quite the same again.

Jerome Bruner's *The Process of Education* confirmed what I had already discovered in a first grade classroom—any subject, at some level of understanding, can be taught to children of all ages. When an infant learns that the ball is round he has begun the study of geometry.

A.J. Nok's book *Memoirs of a Superfluous Man* had a healthy irreverence about many things, learning among them. He helped me lay to rest the notion that "the right answer" is always the most important thing. He also had a kind word for educational elitism, an important fact of life that Americans persist in feeling squeamish about.

My "cause" became helping young people to discover the adventure of learning, and the sheer pleasure of it. It was always that for me; it still is, and my modus operandi as a teacher was always with that in mind. I have taught every age group from nursery school to senior American history, but first grade was always my favorite. For the youngsters I worked with the love of learning was still so spontaneous, so untarnished, there was virtually nothing that didn't pique their curiosity. They weren't afraid to be wrong, and they didn't learn in little boxes—everything was relevant. This is where the line is drawn, the terrible difference between rich and poor. The children of suburbia can be just as full of hell, and just as devious as any other children—in spite of all the good stuff Mom has told them. But they are excited by life. They have been praised, and urged to walk a few steps farther. They believe if they get involved they can make something happen, and they can't wait to see what the something may be.

Reading is a pleasure that has enriched my life, and it was one that I shared with Hy from the very beginning. His first gift to me was a book. We didn't have the same favorite books, but then we were two such different people. I reread *The Brothers Karamazov*, and everything by Loren Eiseley and Edna St. Vincent Millay. He reread Gibbons and everything by Churchill.

Dostoevsky's passage from *The Brothers Karamazov* about the Grand Inquisitor I have read and reread many times, sometimes as the Grand Inquisitor, bearing the truth alone and keeping the masses content; sometimes as the masses, wishing someone on high would toss me a comforting lie. I used to say to my husband, "What will it be like ten years from now, Jim? Where will we be? How will we grow? Lie to me a little. Let's pretend."

But my very honest, very logical, very pedantic husband wouldn't do it. Couldn't do it. Now, I live in a world of perjury, lies and dissembling, where truth is often ignored or sneered at, where it is actually despised by some. "You'll never be happy, Jean, because you don't know what you want." Ah, those moments that come home to roost.

As for Edna St. Vincent Millay, every woman must find herself somewhere in those poems. And every man would find someone he has loved there if he bothered to look. I don't think she is read much in English classes today. She isn't abstruse. You don't have to read the footnotes to figure out what she means. I have wiped my tears on the corner of my apron, and thought of Penelope, "Penelope who really cried." I sat on the side of my bed holding a bouquet of flowers that last night, while Hy hugged his pillow and said he wouldn't talk, and remembered:

> Love in the open hand, no thing but that,
> Ungemmed, unbidden, wishing not to hurt,
> As one should bring you cowslips in a hat
> Swung from the hand, or apples in her skirt

> I bring, you calling out as children do,
> Look what I have—And these are all for you.

It was the last line I had always loved especially. I didn't know until Hy had died it was from a collection of her poems called "Fatal Interview."

I love humorous books and I laugh readily. I am told that a true sense of humor means seeing ourselves as others see us. I am not able to do that, although there are people who find me "funny." My humor, for want of a better word, usually consists of saying something ridiculous about myself before someone else beats me to it. I have no conception at all of how others see me. When from time to time I am forced to hear, it often leaves me shaken, or puzzled, or hurt, and always eager to avoid hearing more. And for reasons that I don't pretend to understand, kindness or praise leaves me far more shaken than unkindness.

Both Hy and I had wonderfully eclectic collections of books. Neither of us read many novels, though I enjoyed some of them more than Hy did. I think he felt his reading time was wasted if he didn't finish a book knowing something specific he hadn't known before; the difference between the Sunni and Shiite Moslems; the history of guerrilla warfare; the history of China; the origin of the Jewish tribes. This sort of thing excited his interest. Character development in a novel was something he didn't have the patience to think about, and too much stuff about inter-personal relations was "silly as hell." The one magazine he always read and enjoyed was *Encounter*, a British monthly. He used to mark things for me to be sure to read and finally he just gave me a subscription.

After Hy had died and his house was sold, my lawyer and I were permitted to go back to examine his room. Everything was changed. Everything was gone—except his books! The big coffee-table-things he never read were gone. Someone took the Harvard classics, but the others, the ones he loved and read and reread had all been left behind.

The books that sat for years right over his bed because he reached for them so often are still sitting there. It made me realize in the starkest possible way that the man I had known and loved, and the man others had known and professed to love, were two quite different people. His books would have been the first thing I'd have packed. It was heart wrenching, standing there in his bedroom, answering a lawyer's questions, trying to be helpful, trying not to see how much of him was still there in the room. I wanted to take the books over his bed and sweep them up in my arms and run away with them. But they belong to strangers now.

New York:
The Fateful Year

1.

The last significant learning epiphany of my intellectual life, if it can be called that, before I sat in a court room, that is, and learned about justice, came in 1966, a watershed year for me—the end of one life and the beginning of another.

I was divorced after almost twenty years of marriage, and left Grosse Pointe, Michigan, where I had lived those years, and with my sons David and Jim, moved to Philadelphia. I stopped being a full-time teacher and became a school administrator, unable to turn down the head-turning salary of $10,000 a year. I began to investigate a new course called "Man: A Course of Study," and on December 9th of that fateful year, I met Dr. Herman Tarnower. It was knowing and loving Hy that ultimately brought me to prison. It was that long ago course that has helped me to survive in prison, and to see with a certain amount of clarity what is going on around me.

"Epiphany," Webster's tells me, is an "intuitive

grasp of reality through something simple and striking." My reaction to the course was exactly that. The course had begun to take shape in 1963 when a group of teachers and social scientists from all over the country met to consider ways to improve the teaching of "social studies"—a junk term that meant a little of anything. Units like "My Friend the Policeman," or "My Friend the Grocer," were boringly predictable, and they didn't get to the heart of the matter, which is humanness. "What is human about a human being? How did he get that way? How can he become more so?" were the questions around which the course was built. With the help of anthropologists like Donald Oliver, Irven deVore, Niko Tinbergen, Konrad Lorenz, the course took shape. Jerome Bruner took a year's leave of absence from his position as head of the Center for Cognitive Studies at Harvard to head the project.

To create the course, which was directed at children in the fifth grade, but is appropriate for all ages, meant giving children access to materials about animal groups and simple human societies, studies that were just then giving birth to the new science of ethology. Ten years later Tinbergen and Lorenz shared the Nobel prize for science with Karl von Frisch. It was the first time that ethology had been so recognized.

There are many themes woven through the course: What is learned and what is innate behavior? How does the structure of our bodies determine our behavior? Why are human babies born so helpless? What role does our dependency upon our parents play in shaping the creatures we become? What are some of the patterns of behavior in the relationship between children and adults? What are cultural behavior patterns and what are individual behavior patterns?

70

Why is learning the human imperative? How does learning increase our range of options and adaptive behavior? What is "acceptable behavior" and how do we decide?

It is difficult to explain how deeply this course affected my thinking and my teaching and my living. It certainly made living more interesting to me, and enriched all my travels. I was much more tolerant of other cultural values and behavior after I had taught the course, and I finally understood W. H. Auden's line, "You shall love your crooked neighbor with your crooked love."

The teachers' manual observes, "We hope the students will gain a new perspective on themselves and the culture they share through an understanding of another way of life, and that they will develop a vocabulary for thinking about the human condition in ways that will assist them in coping with the immense cultural distances that divide the modern world."

What better preparation could one have for going to prison?

I met Hy at a dinner party that Marge and Leslie Jacobson gave. Marge had called me and said, "Jean, there's someone I want you to meet. He's a bright, interesting man, you'd be great together. You like the same things." I was living in Philadelphia by then. David and Jim were at Chestnut Hill Academy and I was working right next door as director of the Middle School at Springside. My father always called it "Springdale or whatever." A trip to New York, even including Marge and Leslie's hospitality was a big budget item, and I gave it some thought. Should I go all the way to New York for a dinner party? Before it began, that dinner party was a "special occasion,"

71

and almost from the moment it ended, my life became "a special occasion."

I don't know who else came to the party, but I remember Hy and me sitting on a sofa talking the evening away, interested, enjoying one another, showing off about our recent trips to Russia, trying to be clever and laughing at ourselves as we were to do so many times again. At 11:00 P.M. sharp with the party in full swing, a bell rang: Henri van der Vreken, Hy's chauffeur, had arrived for Dr. Tarnower. Hy rose, said his goodbyes, and like Cinderella, bid a hasty retreat. I hadn't yet learned that leaving the party early was Hy's custom, and nothing and nobody would ever change it.

I was disappointed to see him go: I thought he had been enjoying the evening as much as I, and I went to bed thinking I would probably never see him again. A few weeks later he sent me a copy of Yaguel Yadin's book *Masada* with a card that read, "It's time you learned more about the Jews, Hy Tarnower." His Christmas note was more traditional and read, "You were a delight to be with. I kept wondering if you could keep up the pace."

I wrote and thanked him for the book and said it had arrived at a perfect time because I was in the hospital for minor surgery. He responded at once with a dozen red roses. For the next two years he must have supported a florist in Germantown who delivered dozens and dozens of roses. They were there waiting for me when I came back from New York; they were there when I couldn't get to New York; they were there cheering me, warming me, wooing me, watching me fall completely in love with the sender. And it wasn't the sound of one hand clapping, for Hy was falling in love too.

He hardly overwhelmed me with attention after the

Christmas card. Hy moved, as he would always move, in his own good time. He was always on time for everything, but he never rushed. He walked slowly, "the cardiac shuffle" he called it. He planned his next move well ahead of time, and when it suited his purpose he had the patience of Job. Finally he wrote. He had planned a safari in Kenya that February and would be back the first week in March. Was there any chance I might be in New York that week? There was. I would be attending meetings of the National Association of Independent Schools.

I left the Friday afternoon meetings early to buy a pair of black shoes at I. Miller—splurging. I still have the damned shoes—they've worn better than I did. Hy picked me up at the Barbizon Plaza at 7:00 P.M., Henri driving the big blue Cadillac which looked to me, seven Cadillacs later, like the one he was driving the day he died. His explanation: "You know what people think of Jewish doctors who drive big Cadillacs. I enjoy a new car but I don't enjoy advertising the fact that I have one."

We had dinner at one of those little New York restaurants where you order something special, ahead of time, and the chef comes out and tells you he hopes you enjoyed it. Hy beamed happily. He was like a kid with a new girl. The months before we met had been lonely ones for him. His constant companion had grown weary of waiting for a wedding ring and had left him to marry someone else. Other women had done the same thing over the years, but this one had upset him deeply. He was fifty-six years old, approaching the point of no return. He still believed that the complete social acceptance he ached for required marriage, and he still couldn't bring himself to make that commitment.

You might say Mrs. Harris dropped by while the

73

doctor was nursing a broken heart—cracked anyway. But his powers of recovery were splendid. I didn't know until after Hy died that as soon as her marriage failed the old friend was back on his doorstep—the door to his bedroom that is, furious to find that I had entered the picture. Apparently the anger has never subsided. She is one of the few people who has vented her wrath through the media, making outrageous statements about me, a woman whom she has never even met and one who for many years felt a kinship and concern for her.

After I was convicted of murdering Hy and had been sent to prison, I received this letter:

> I was Dr. Tarnower's lover before he met you. He couldn't possibly have hurt you any more than he hurt me, but I wouldn't have murdered the man.
>
> His friends and I are glad that you are in prison, and we hope you die there.

I don't know who the author is, or where she came in the pecking order of Herman's playmates, but she isn't one of my favorites, whoever she is. I realize now, as I take the time to think about it, that the question is not why I fell in love with Hy, but what in the name of God he saw in me. What needs did I fill in the world he aspired to live in?

We left the restaurant and headed for the bar at the Pierre, a favorite place of mine ever since. Hy had two Manhattans, almost unheard of for him; I had two whiskey sours, almost unheard of for me. We talked about politics. I had met Richard Nixon a few weeks before at a dinner party in Philadelphia, and remember predicting that they certainly couldn't seriously consider running him for president. But most of the time we danced. Hy was a marvelous dancer, "The sine qua non of bachelorhood" he laughed. He was graceful and full of rhythm. The stuffy side of him, and there was a very stuffy side, was left behind when he danced. The stuffy side of me, and there is a very stuffy side, was left behind when I danced with Hy.

Years later when we were dancing at the Century Country Club one night, and I felt as I always did when I danced with Hy—sailing two feet off the floor—he said, "You know, you're a helluva good dancer. But you sure were stiff as a board when I first met you." This didn't come as a surprise. My husband had always said in a half teasing, half serious way, "Okay sweetie pie. Let's have the duty dance."

Two weeks after our first date was spring vacation, and the boys and I went to New York for the weekend. Friday night I took them to see *Mame*, their first New York play. Saturday night old friends of Hy's gave a dinner party for his fifty-seventh birthday. It was the first of thirteen birthdays I would celebrate with him. We celebrated it in Nepal, in Hong Kong, in Hawaii, the Bahamas, Purchase, all over the world. It wasn't until eight years later that Hy discovered when my birthday was—quite by accident. He never asked and I never told him.

That Sunday the boys and I drove to Hy's house for lunch. I still remember the curried shrimp. It was my first glimpse of the house on Purchase Street, a place that was like home to me for many years.

I visited Hy three or four times in the next two months. He came to Philadelphia, he called every evening at 6:30, he wrote and sent flowers. I stayed at Hy's friends Arthur and Vivian Schulte's house in Armonk when I came. The largest problem was seldom being alone with him.

Hy loved to give and go to dinner parties. I didn't.

75

One weekend when he had promised we wouldn't go to any, I arrived to find Saturday night booked with a dinner party so fancy he hadn't been able to bring himself to refuse. We took a long walk that afternoon, sat on a hilltop where we could look out over Long Island Sound, and later, as he drove off to dinner, I drove back to Philadelphia.

I learned very early on that dinner with the Wasps in Grosse Pointe and dinner with "Our Crowd" in New York involved very different rituals. The two groups worshipped different idols. In Grosse Pointe it was the martinis. In New York it was the food. Dinner was later in Grosse Pointe because of the martinis—but mercifully people drank them instead of talking about them. In New York they talked about the food. In my entire life I had never heard food and the preparation of it so thoroughly and so constantly discussed. "Was the cook good? Was the cook hopeless? Wasn't it ghastly trying to find a new one? Did you ever have better bird's nest soup? Is the bouillabaisse as good as it was in the darling little restaurant down in Rio?"

I'm not a bad cook. At least I was once not a bad cook. My stuffed peppers, pot roast, egg dishes, shepherd's pie, and blueberry pie were darned good. I don't think I could rustle them up today. Every single time for fourteen years that we sat down to eat with Hy's closest friends, Arthur and Vivian Schulte, the subject was always whether Vivian like the food, and whether it was half as good as she could have prepared it herself. She even tasted the food on your plate that you ordered in a restaurant and told you if that had been properly prepared too. Since the Schultes were hosts to me many times, or hosts to Hy, with me the broad-he-brought, I sound ungrateful and I don't mean to. But those meals left a lasting scar.

Vivian and Arthur came to my house for a meal only once. They came to Philadelphia to visit old friends and I invited them for Sunday brunch. Having done so I then proceeded to wish I hadn't because I realized that I was terrified. Vivian was a food expert, and Arthur had a long list of stuff he absolutely had to have or absolutely couldn't have and I hadn't mastered the list. I asked Mary, one of the maids who worked at Springside, if she would come and help and she graciously agreed.

The guests arrived, the Schultes and their friends, and some of us had Bloody Mary's and Arthur had his usual Scotch and water. We nibbled some good smoked salmon with our drinks. Lunch started with soup because Arthur likes soup. It was gazpacho as I recall because the boys liked my gazpacho. I hadn't told Mary anything about pouring wine because I intended to do that myself. But in between courses, while I was talking instead of listening, Mary came in looking like something out of a William Powell movie, with a white linen napkin wrapped around what I assumed was the wine. She proceeded to pour and I continued to talk.

Suddenly there was a rather awkward silence and Arthur said, "Jean, did you really mean for all of us to have a glassful of Scotch with lunch?" If there had been any ice, that pretty well took care of it, and I relaxed and enjoyed the rest of the meal. Vivian was kind and never gave me a run-down on how it could have been improved, though she probably had a long run-down tucked away.

Over the years I have developed such a deep-seated feeling of inadequacy about cooking that I quake at the threshold of the kitchen. I baked thousands of cookies for the girls at Madeira—but usually late at night when no one was looking. And to kids at boarding school a chocolate chip cookie is a chocolate chip cookie. I not only never prepared birds' nest soup, in my heart of hearts I have never even harbored a desire to prepare it. I can miss a meal without missing it, and by and large I like to be able to identify what's on my plate instead of guessing or having someone tell me. Right from the start I was something of a misfit in old Herm's life, and he was certainly a misfit in mine, but that was part of the attraction.

"Well he can certainly do without her," I heard the hostess say with feeling to one of the other dinner guests. I was the "her." It was the first time I had been there for dinner, though there were many other dinners to follow. The conversation had centered for quite some time on the problems of giving your children their inheritance while you were still alive, or waiting for the will. One concerned father said his daughter was spending it so fast she'd have it all used up by the time he died. Didn't this possibility worry the hostess? "No way, darling," she said. "There is no way they can spend it all in my lifetime."

Brooke Astor was one of the guests that night, a charming lady as I recall. "She's richer than Croesus, darling, and believe me she earned every bit of it the hard way. He was a perfect bastard." It was a Noel Coward play and my part hadn't quite jelled in the author's mind—or I had come in before my cue. I wasn't intimidated. Human attitudes and poses fascinate me. I was a deeply appreciative audience, but my natural candor was showing, and the lines I made up for myself had the ring of an outsider, someone who didn't take the problems under discussion seriously enough. "I don't know where he found her but he can certainly do without her."

Hy wrote his script very well on these occasions. That little Jewish boy from Brooklyn could wing it with "Our Crowd" and leave them begging for more. And he loved being there, rubbing elbows with people who had lived with big money for generations. None of this "well-to-do" garbage—rich, really rich, that's what he loved. It was the ultimate redeeming feature as far as Hy was concerned. If you were going to be rude, if you weren't very bright, if you came late to one of his dinner parties, you better damned well be rich.

My friends never said it within my hearing, but the message of their polite silence after they had met Hy came through loud and clear. "What on earth does she see in him? Jean, of all people, giving up hearth and home for that." My mother was never judgmental or unkind about something she at best would never understand, but she did say finally, "Dear, when you write to Dad and me please, don't mention Hy's name." To each his own. Who can say what attracts people to one another? I guess you have to know and understand their needs first. Love, like happiness, doesn't come ready-made. It has to be made to order.

Within the next two months after I met him, Hy had asked me to marry him and had given me a beautiful ring, a four-carat diamond.

I told Springside that I would be leaving to get married, and since the timing was poor they were annoyed: A member of the Springside administration had met Hy at lunch once and said, "He'll never marry you. I know his type, and I know Jews."

That was pretty much the end of any rapport that she and I had. Later, Hy broke the engagement and I stayed on at Springside. The following year, the same woman turned to me over her third bourbon one night and said, "They'll never make you headmistress now.

Everyone knows you're been living with a Jew." Nothing I experienced in those fourteen years brought me closer to Hy than that, though it was an experience I never shared with him. When I told a member of the board what had been said his answer was classic. "Oh, I'm sure you must be mistaken. Why some of my best friends are Jews."

After Hy had died, several of his friends and relatives suggested to the press that Mrs. Harris had probably gotten her job at Madeira through "the doctor's influence" or "one of his friends." How wonderfully naive. How positively American. Loving a Jewish doctor is not the royal road to the headship of a private school. But there was never a job I wouldn't happily have bypassed if the alternative had been not seeing Hy.

2.

We went to Jamaica that first winter for a week, and then out West the following September. In between we saw little of each other and went about our own particular lives. Mine consisted of being mother, housekeeper, and a very hard-working teacher and administrator. Hy's consisted of being a very conscientious doctor and having one helluva good time. We had thought that summer would be marrying time.

The day that Hy called to tell me he couldn't go through with the marriage wins handily as the second worst day in my life. I had rented a wonderful old house in Philadelphia for the boys and me. It was very old; it had seven fireplaces, lots of atmosphere, and squirrels in the attic and funny sounds in the walls. I woke that fateful morning in my full-of-atmosphere bedroom and saw something gray moving up the wall; I watched, fascinated. It could have been a shadow. Then suddenly I looked down and noticed another gray shadow moving across the floor where the dog always slept. I got out of bed to investigate and the gray shadow was tiny ticks, hundreds and hundreds of ticks, moving slowly across the room and up the wall!

The sight of one tick disgusts me. It is only love of a dog that gives me the courage to touch one. This was a Hitchcock movie "The Ticks!" I rushed to the Yellow Pages to find an exterminator, dialed, and a friendly voice assured me I had come to the right place and he would be there today. He told me ticks can lay eggs in woodwork and the eggs can lie dormant for years. Then when a new host dog appears, overnight they can burst into bloom. He added, very discreetly, that his truck had no lettering on it so the neighbors wouldn't know the exterminators were there. I assured him he could come with signs and sirens, just get there.

While I waited I swept up ticks with broom and dustpan. Then, as I stooped over to pick up a wastebasket, my back, which hadn't gone out for years, suddenly snapped and a sharp pain tore through my whole body. I managed to crawl to my bed and drag myself up on it. It was while I lay there, tears streaming down my cheeks because of the pain, heaps of unswept ticks still crawling past the broom and dustpan, that Hy called to have a heart-to-heart talk about how he thought it was late in the day for him to play the role of husband and father, and he didn't think he could go through with it. I felt like Job in drag.

"Now I don't know which part of me hurts the most," I cried—and burst into tears all over again.

Hy's roses arrived that afternoon just before the exterminator. With Jimmy clutching the dog's leash and everyone's toothbrush, and me clutching the roses, and David carrying the houseplants I managed to crawl into a friend's car and she took us home with her for the night while the exterminator did in the ticks and whatever was making noise in the walls. I wrapped up the ring that night and sent it back to Hy with a caustic suggestion that he give it to Suzanne van der Vrecken, his cook, since she was the only woman he really needed or wanted to hang on to. The next day I was fitted with a special corset that I had to wear part of the time for next five years. And Hy did what he always did, went about the business of living his life pretty much as he wanted to, and I went about the business of doing what I would always do, loving him.

In less than a week the ring was back with a note that said, "It's yours forever, darling. If you won't wear it, save it for David." And with it came a bottle of Percobarb, ostensibly for the pain in my back. At first Hy said, "We can't see each other anymore. You're a wonderful woman, Jean, and you ought to be married. What I have to offer isn't for you." He could have carried it off. I couldn't.

After I had come to terms with the reality of his inability to marry, it was I who wrote the reassuring letter. In some ways Hy was more concerned about it than I was. It indicated a weakness in him that he found hard to come to terms with. Later on, about five years later, he was comfortable with, "Well, I married my profession." But at age fifty-seven he knew that wasn't the only reason and it troubled him. He still cherished all the middle-class values—I'm glad I knew him then—and felt that full respectability and social acceptance required marriage. He also harbored the frightening suspicion, which he voiced from time to time, that people might think he was a homosexual because he hadn't married.

By the time Hy and I met, I was forty-two and Hy was fifty-six. The sociological reasons for marriage, nesting and raising the young, were past. The reason now was to enjoy the companionship of someone you loved. Enjoying the "social security" a woman feels when the man at her side is her husband is pleasant too, but not reason enough to walk away from love and "get married." My friendship with Hy was a monument to my conviction that a very true love is more important than loneliness, and certainly more important than "what people think" when no pledges or commitments are being broken, and no one else is being hurt.

Hy's friends, some who grew fond of me over the years, used to take me aside at dinner parties and say, "Jean, why don't you give up. You ought to be married, and he's never going to get married." I think many of them thought I was hanging on, just in case. I never for a moment thought he would change his mind—he couldn't—and I never felt any loss of integrity because we didn't marry.

It was sometime in early 1970 that Hy called to tell me he thought he was going to marry a woman with four children. I was standing at the phone in the kitchen when he called, and I can remember saying to him, "Herman Tarnower, I know and you *should* know that you aren't going to marry anyone. So why don't you stop hurting so many women, and just concentrate on hurting me." He seemed to enjoy that line. I loved his hearty laugh.

From that moment on we saw more and more of one another, and when I finally moved to Connecticut in 1971 we spent almost every weekend together until

I moved to Virginia in 1977. Before I reached Connecticut, however, there was a second lady with another four children that he took a careful look at too. I've never quite figured out how he worked in both of them in that short space of time, but he did. To misuse a metaphor, there was never any grass growing under Herman's feet.

Without the opportunity to get completely away from Hy's social life our relationship, whatever it was, however one chooses to label it, would never have happened. It was only when we were alone, at home or away, that Hy was the very special person I fell in love with. There was a beautiful little pond in front of his house with a small island in the middle. I loved walking around the pond with him. He was proud of having created it out of a swamp. He knew every forget-me-not, buttercup, iris, waterlily, cattail that grew beside it. He had planted many of them himself, and he smiled at each one as we walked arm in arm beside them. My last birthday gift to Hy for his seventieth, which he didn't live to enjoy, was some lily bulbs for beside the pond. He had orange and yellow ones. I had added ten more colors.

If I could relive only one time in our lives together it would be a Sunday afternoon, one of two: a Sunday walking slowly around the pond and then up the hill to check the old peach tree and the wild raspberries in the back of the property — or it would be a Sunday afternoon at a small dacha about twenty miles outside of Warsaw, where we went for lunch at the home of a Polish surgeon whom Dr. Howard Rusk had introduced us to. The dining room had French doors opening on to a late September garden. I remember sitting there listening as our host talked about Poland in the years since the war. His daughter and I took turns making occasional trips to the kitchen, and the conversation went on for several hours.

The late afternoon sun came through the lacy old curtains at the windows in such a special way that time stood still for a while, and I knew that for some hard to explain reason I would remember the moment all my life. I was far away from home, but Hy was there, and the light through the window reminded me of a scene from a Pasternak story, or of home when I was a little girl. I loved Hy for being part of the moment and for giving the moment to me. It was nine years ago and I can feel it and hear it and see it and smell it still. It is a physical part of me. What difference do the why's make? It just is.

3.

Our first trip to Palm Springs was short and happy, and memorable for another reason. I walked into Saks for some black-and-white shoes while we were there and found exactly what I was looking for. Hy was there with me and when I went to give the saleswoman my charge plate Hy had already paid for them. I was traveling with a man who wasn't my husband without even the slightest tinge of guilt or feeling of impropriety, but having him pay for a pair of my shoes embarrassed me. I never wore them without remembering and feeling self-conscious.

The lines between etiquette, morality, respectability and manners are dimly drawn, though each is quite different. We each choose our own particular niceties to give priority to, always trying to separate the specious from the real thing. Over the years Hy gave me some lovely gifts, expensive gifts I suppose, but having him buy my clothes smacked to me of being "kept," something I did not wish to be, and never was. Except for a Liberty scarf, and a cotton skirt he insisted upon giving me because he bought a similar one for our hostess in St. Martin, Hy did not ever buy my clothes.

I discovered, years later, during the trial, that his friends and family apparently thought that he had paid many of my bills. He didn't. And that was the way we both wanted it. From the moment I fell in love with Hy the only thing that mattered was seeing him, when I reasonably could. Never seeing him was the price I couldn't pay. I picked up all the other tabs, social, professional, and some rather steep financial ones with no regret.

That one of Hy's friends should suggest to the newspapers that he had probably helped pay for my sons' education enraged me. I would never have permitted it, the boys wouldn't have wanted it, and Hy would never have suggested it. Besides, I was very proud that I did it myself. It wasn't easy. That anyone would suggest it is an indication of how little he had tried to know me. Hy did offer to send Jim to a camp in Europe one summer. I thanked him and declined. When Jim finally went abroad he worked his way over on a freighter.

It was when we put New York behind us and traveled that Hy was at his best, a best many people never saw. He was a perfect traveling companion, bright, funny, never tired, well informed about what he was going to see, never complaining, determined not to let the normal annoyances of travel make a difference. The happiness, the exhilaration of our trips together are something I could not exaggerate.

Hy would arrive at the airport smiling and taking charge, and I became the happy follower, a role quite foreign to me in my day to day life, but one I played most willingly with him. There was friendship and companionship and sharing the sheer joy of touching another part of the world, shaking ourselves free of the small boxes we all seem to live in most of our lives. We read, we reached out to one another and to new experiences, and we learned. When we returned we were never quite the same people again. Maybe it's presumptuous to speak for Hy. I know I wasn't the same again. We understood a little more, cared a little more. Places we had hardly heard of before became important to us, and so did the people who lived there.

There was one drawback, but I learned to live with it. It never seemed "wrong" to me for us to be together. I felt no need for moral false faces. Hy wasn't as open and honest as I, but then his life was much more complicated than mine. He could seem open and ingenuous when he was being most secretive. He wrote many "dear all" letters as he traveled around the world with me beside him, but he never mentioned my name. I don't know whether that was to protect my privacy or his, but I imagine it was the latter.

That way he could send letters to all the ladies on the "dear all" list without any deletions or complications. I couldn't have written about those trips without mentioning him. It was sharing the pleasure of them with him that made them so special. He acted as though he felt the same way, but when he wrote the letters he could lift me out of the picture with no effort at all. I was shifted from person to nonperson very quickly. As with so many unpleasantries I was hurt for a moment, and then forgot about it in a rush of new adventures.

We ran the gamut from a suite at the Ritz in Paris to a crowded buggy little room in Varna, a Bulgarian town on the Black Sea coast; from the American

Embassy in New Delhi to a tiny ranch house in Montana; from a splendid room overlooking the bay in Hong Kong to a place in Khartoum where we sprayed everything with Lysol and sat out on a terrace until late at night, sipping tea and putting off the moment when we went inside; from sipping champagne in first class on Pan Am to wrapping ourselves in sweaters and jackets on the deck of a dangerously overcrowded ferry between Iraklion and Piraeus, sharing two oranges, a package of biscuits, and a bottle of Manhattans for dinner and breakfast.

We bought wine and bread and cheese and sat in the sun and the wind at Knossos, reading the guide book and then winding our way through the labyrinth. There was a wind from the Sahara, you could feel the sand from all those miles away, but the sun was warm. It was early spring. Early March was usually when spring vacation came, and that meant we were often lucky enough to arrive before the spring flowers had been trampled. Indeed, in many instances we visited places before tourists had taken much notice of them: Bali, Nepal, Burma, Afghanistan, Bahrain, Jiddah, N'Gor, and many, many others.

We wakened at daybreak in Kandy in central Ceylon, to the beating of the drums at the Temple of the Tooth; we watched from the terrace of a small rest house in Ratnapura, while hundreds of monkeys swung from the trees and finally settled down for the night and returned to our room where netting covered the beds and a large lazy fan in the ceiling provided more noise than air. We flew into Kabul, that city in the land of Cain, with snow on the mountains and almond trees in bloom, and savagery just below the surface. It was more than a different place; it was a different moment in time, a scene from the Middle

Ages.

Trips with Hy, or just visits with Hy, were the times I breathed free for a little while and thought about something more than my next move, or how to placate the next irate constituent. I became a thinking, feeling person again with horizons broader than the walls of an office. The very word "mankind" became something more than statistics on a page or a sound made by teachers. Thanks to Hy, the word "mankind" has become a kaleidoscope of pictures for me.

It's the women in Afghanistan picking up twigs along a dusty road where a stick five or six inches long is a treasure—and they do it every day for firewood and cooking! It is the women of Senegal standing tall and stylishly decked out in bright gowns and headdresses, balancing large bundles on their heads. It is the women of Kenya who carry heavy bundles on their backs with the help of a strap that goes across their foreheads; the young woman with a deep indentation across the forehead is considered very marriageable; it is a badge of honor, proof positive that she is a good beast of burden. It's the man with a Ph.D. in geology from the University of New Mexico who married a Nepalese woman from a small mountain village where men go down into the valley twice a year for salt and cloth. It's an old gentleman in Kenya, late of Her Majesty's Indian Army "till they closed India down"; complete with khaki shorts and monocle, reminiscing "Mahvelous duty, that. Everything so cheap, you know, whiskey, tennis balls."

It is the hundreds of children in Ceylon, spilling out of little thatched cottages in spotless white dresses and shirts, on their way to school. It's the hundreds of young men in Ceylon, Kenya, Senegal, and so many other places, who have just enough education to feel disdainful of their old ways of life, and are quite incapable of making a living in a new way of life; it is the young Burmese doctors who will graduate this year from medical schools into an economy that can support only a handful of them. The rest will join cadres of workers out in the country, working for food and shelter, struggling through the years of red tape that may in time bring them to America.

It is gypsies making their way through the Khyber Pass in bright painted wagons like the pictures in my fifth grade geography book. It's the jovial Franciscan monk who showed us through the archaeological digs on the island of Bahrain, and the sheik who governs that rich, strategic island, he of the Salukis and Persian carpets and falcons and private beaches for his "girls." I don't think it's called a harem any more.

It's the women who threw their babies away with the trash in the unmercifully crowded refugee camps in Saigon, or the boy on the streets of that city who pulled an old sleight-of-hand trick while exchanging dollars for piastres and left Hy with a package of folded newspapers. Hy laughed and said, "Well, he outsmarted me." Later he added; "Don't you tell Arthur." I thought of the two of them that day at Madeira when I discovered that many of the girls had been using a stranger's charge card to make phone calls all over the world. "There's no such thing as a free lunch, my friends," I told them, "but all your life someone will offer you one."

Only once in all our travels did Hy ever get angry with me, at least so that I knew, and the anger was strange and deep, and left me cowering like a wounded rabbit for twenty-four miserable hours. I was in Rome. The concierge had told him he couldn't get us reservations for dinner at the place Hy had named. He looked disappointed, and I wanted him to know that anywhere we went was splendid with me. "Oh, well, let's try . . ." and I named another restaurant. "Goddammit!" he shouted. "Are you running this, or am I? If you want to run things, just let me know, and I'll turn it over to you. Just take over or shut up!"

He sulked and was angry that night and all the next day. I was accustomed to that behavior in my father. He never took a trip that wasn't four parts yelling to one part enjoyment, but I was spoiled now by Hy's good spirits and kindness. Jolly thing, kindness. One is never happier than when other people are good. I wouldn't have angered him for the world, but I did, and it terrified me. I was like a child wanting to put things right again, and probably annoying him all the more because I cared so much.

Only once in all our travels did I ever get angry with him. It wasn't until we reached the Ritz in Paris in 1976 that I realized the letters that had followed us around the world for years were from Lynne Tryforos. I had said to him in Hawaii in 1972 when we picked up the mail and he fumbled around awkwardly trying to hide what became very familiar handwriting, "Hy, why would you travel with me if you give your itinerary to another woman?" He did not enjoy being asked for explanations, and he answered with obvious annoyance. "Look, dear, they have it at the office. There's nothing I can do. It's just a little note from one of the girls at the office."

In Paris the letter had been slipped under the door of our room, and was waiting for us when we arrived. It was my first trip to Paris, and laden with all the old stereotypes; I had even bought that first black nightgown for the occasion. We had been gone almost three weeks, through eastern Europe, and were ending the trip in Paris. It had been an exceptionally interesting

91

and happy time. Now the first thing that greeted us was Lynne's letter. It looked like a twenty-page term paper. Again it was quickly and awkwardly whisked away. I said nothing. A few moments later, while Hy was dressing for dinner, I walked over to the mantle and started to put my pearls and earrings down where Hy had laid some cuff links. They were ones he had had for several years, "From a grateful patient."

He had put them face down, and there staring at me, engraved in gold, was all Lynne's love. The pleasure of Paris were pretty well laid to rest, and I was angry enough to slam a closet door very hard. As I did, the floor to ceiling mirror on it shattered all over the room. I hadn't expected that, but I wasn't sorry.

Hy reacted as if nothing had happened. He simply ignored it. He apologized for the letter and for bringing the cuff links, asked me if I was ready for dinner, and we headed for the Crazy Horse Saloon—a terrible place! By the time we returned, the mirror had been replaced, and there wasn't the smallest chip of glass on the floor to indicate anything had been amiss. Two years later, when friends who had just returned from Paris were moaning about how expensive breakfast was at the Ritz, Hy smiled at me and said very quietly, "Their mirrors are damned expensive, too." That's the only reference he ever made to it.

I used to say to him, especially when he was beginning to talk about another trip and ask me where I'd like to go, "You know, Herm, we don't have to go far. I could be very happy with you on the Staten Island Ferry." Hy didn't respond to the Staten Island comment at the time; but years later, when the sun was just going down and the lights of Hong Kong were beginning to sparkle in a hundred different colors on the water, we stood on the deck of the ferry to Kowloon and he said, "It's taken a long time, but I finally got you on the Staten Island Ferry."

Brooklyn:
Hy

1.

For fourteen years Hy had been "there," filling my life, being bright, being difficult, being thoughtful, being selfish, letting the world think he was being any damned thing he chose to be, but carrying burdens and scars I have only now begun to acknowledge. He was the kind of man you were attracted to, or you probably couldn't stand—no middle ground, and he felt the same way about you. If he found you interesting, or useful, he was a good friend, or useful in return. If he didn't like you, you could go to hell.

It would be difficult to describe the nature of our relationship. I'm not sure what it was myself, what made him so important to me, what attracted me to him. The forensic psychologist who tested me for more than nineteen hours after Hy's death wrote:

I feel that this patient in the years since 1966 seemed to live what Dr. Menninger would describe as "a partial death and substitute for suicide." She had truncated her life through her subjection to Dr. Tarnower in such a manner as to kill part of herself in masochistic surrender. She had recurring bouts of depression as she realized that she could not free herself from the man . . . who denied her status, sadistically teased her, and was a figure of complicity in her long standing, self-destructive vulnerability.

If true, and I'm still not the best judge, it was certainly something neither Hy nor I planned or wanted, Hy least of all.

My own strong conviction is that I would have resorted to suicide long before if Hy hadn't been there saying, "Welcome home, darling," and teaching me how to enjoy life, or at least letting me watch him enjoy it. Saul Bellow, in a short story called "A Silver Dish," wrote, "It's usually the selfish people who are loved the most. They do what you deny yourself, and you love them for it."

Like all of us, Hy was a mixture of good and bad, a distillation of his heritage, his different environments and his own unique self. The story of his life is a success story for men, and a cautionary tale for women. He was not an introspective man. Life is not conducive to reflection today, and that suited Hy just fine. Reflecting was not what he usually enjoyed. Doing, seeing, learning, experiencing now was for him. He worked much harder at enjoying than understanding.

Digging too deep was a bore, or a threat, I'm not sure which. He didn't clutter up his life with peripheral considerations. He got to the main point very quickly, and then had a tendency to oversimplify by making that the only point. Perhaps by trial and error, perhaps by instinct he had found the straightest line between survival and the good life. People who tarried too long over all the possibilities he dismissed as fools. "You're wacky," he was constantly telling me in a smiling, affable way. It was what I expected to hear when I arrived in his bedroom that night in March.

When I think of Hy now (he could never quite remember how he got that nickname), I hear the sound of his footsteps first, on the stairway coming up from the garage. His head appears, and then the rest of him. He's smiling and he says, "Hello" with the accent on the O. "Welcome home." I was usually in the living room reading when he came home, and I would stop my reading and go to kiss him.

I have read descriptions of Hy that sound nothing at all like him to me. People emphasize his nose, and make him sound very severe. I picture beautiful deep brown eyes, a bald head, and a big, broad smile, or a warm private one, with his eyes smiling too. He was just under six feet tall, he kept his weight between 175 and 180, and he was proud of his very flat stomach. My favorite picture of Hy is one Audrey Topping took of him in China in 1973 . . . tie open, carryall in hand, and a smile that said, "I am doing exactly what I want most to do, and I'm loving it." It is Hy at his most ingenuous, something he wasn't always good at being.

The carryall in the picture probably held his shaving kit, his passport and traveler's checks, a few small gifts he had picked up, a sweater, and three good books. If he had lost all his other baggage it wouldn't have dampened his spirits a bit. It usually took him twenty minutes to pack for a world tour, and in the fourteen years that I knew him he always took the same things: three pair of tried khakis, a few drip-dry shirts, sweaters, two pair of the ubiquitous blue pajamas, undershorts, two good shirts, two ties and a suit. He wouldn't have made the best dressed list even

96

in China, but he was comfortable. He wore the clothes. They never wore him.

At home his clothes were very conservative, very good, and they lasted forever. Many of the jackets hanging in Hy's closet had been there for more than fourteen years. He never liked wide lapels or wide ties so he wasn't inconvenienced by passing fads. Suzanne, his cook, asked me every year to make him buy himself a new topcoat but he had the old one relined and some magic performed on the cuffs and wore the same one. Besides, Suzanne knew very well nobody made him do anything.

The last few years of his life he began to get a bit more daring sartorially, especially after friends gave him a bright green sweater when we celebrated one of his birthdays in Palm Springs. His first reaction was that it would have to go back. Then he decided he liked it. He even graduated to a yellow Izod and a pink Izod for golf, and a few handsome striped shirts instead of whites for the office. I always thought he looked wonderful on his way to the office, partly because I like his tweeds and choice of ties, and partly because he always looked refreshed and eager for whatever the new day would bring. He couldn't wait to get started.

Six days a week for almost forty years he was up and on his way to the hospital and then the office by 7:15. I've known him to make three house calls in the middle of the night and still be up and out by 7:15 the next morning. I think he had discovered the fountain of youth . . . good health, work that he loved, and the capacity to play as hard as he worked.

Hy loved being rich, but he was a liberal by nature. He found it hard to be a bigot or to deny something his intellect found obvious. The solution was not to think about troublesome things too long.

97

Hy was a moral man where his medical practice was concerned. He was amoral where women were concerned. I think he was comfortable with the arrangement because he had divided the world into givers and takers, first class and second class, and men were the former and women were the latter.

He simply never questioned that God designed the sexes to occupy different spheres. He wasn't interested in a woman filling the benign roles of wife and mother. On the other hand, if you worked as hard as he did, and I did, it still didn't buy you more than a second-class ticket to life. His behavior swung from the side of grace to the side of hubris, an anomaly I was never equipped to understand fully or cope with intelligently. Instead, I simply endured it, remembering the good parts, loving enough to forgive the bad parts.

As a happy and contented friend he was the most agreeable companion imaginable. As a practicing physician he was bright, intuitive and courageous, always willing and ready to consult, as well as to be consulted. As a member of the profession he was a one-man band, not a member of a committee, not a joiner, not a political animal. There we had something in common. Hy was one of the founders of the Westchester Heart Association, the first chairman of its board and later honorary chairman, but while he never stopped caring about the Association and working for it, he needed to be given a specific job, do it, and be done with it. _

He was not a patient member of any meeting. To be so meant to suffer an occasional fool, and this he never did—not unless there was something much more in it for him than chairmanship of a committee. A year or so before he died he was asked to help find new board members for the Association. I was sitting beside him when he called Oscar Dystel and asked him if he would consider serving. "Hy," Mr. Dystel answered, "I am already a member of the board of the Westchester Heart Association." It was a gaffe that would have shaken and certainly embarrassed anyone else. Hy looked sheepish for a moment—but only a moment.

Hy's tolerance for anything or anyone he didn't like was largely used up on the wives of his two closest friends. He cordially loathed them both. "Jesus! She is impossible" was his constant refrain. They are two intelligent, independent women and very devoted wives. Hy saw them only as women who talked too much. He said one night as we drove home from an evening with both of them, "You know, they are probably the only two people in the world who would have invited Einstein for dinner and corrected him when he started explaining relativity!" By and large he was charming and uncharacteristically long-suffering with them both, because he was devoted to their husbands.

There isn't much to tell about the early history of Hy because for him his history began when he became a doctor. He isn't an easy person to imagine as a child. I loved to hear him reminisce but he didn't do it often, and he rarely went back further than college. I've forgotten some of the particulars; I listened with interest and affection, but always with the comfortable feeling that I'd hear him tell it again. I particularly loved to hear him use an occasional Yiddish word. It was almost always in a light, warm moment, and it gave him roots, whether he wanted them or not.

He didn't seem to remember much that would fall under the heading of "fun" as a youngster. There are few carefree children in Yiddish literature. Maybe he was part of a tradition. He grew up in Brooklyn with his mother and father, and three sisters, Billie, Edith, and Jean. He played the usual street games—stickball, stoop ball, punch ball, handball—all, I imagine, with a ferocious will to win. He fought with his sister Jean—she must have been the one most like him, and played pool whenever he could. On a number of occasions his mother came and pulled him out of a local pool hall. It's a picture I can't quite imagine. "Because it was late or because of the company?" I asked. He smiled, "A little of both, I guess." He never got over loving to gamble, but he never gambled recklessly, and over the long haul I think he was a winner. Framed in his dining room was a royal flush in clubs—trophy of a big night. "It helped to build this house."

Hy's family had very little money. I thought it was wonderful that he had started from nothing and "made it" on his own. His father was in the hat business and made a respectable lower middle-class living until the depression, when people stopped buying hats. Then "we barely scraped by." He always spoke of his father with affection and respect. He was a quiet man while Mama did the talking. "He didn't have much money, but whatever he did have he was generous with. He paid for my college—how the hell he did it, I don't know. He even bought me a little secondhand roadster after I'd been hitchiking for years."

Hitchiking? Dr. Tarnower? My son Jim was incredulous when I told him how Hy hitchhiked across the country one summer during his college years. I think in Jim's mind Hy had slipped out of the womb with the umbilical cord wrapped around a new blue Cadillac. It was just part of the package that was Dr. Tarnower. Herman, without a ticket to Kenya and a

100

handful of graphite fishing poles? Nonsense. No hundred-foot swimming pool? No tennis court? You're thinking of another Dr. Tarnower.

2.

I don't think there was ever a moment in his life when he didn't want all that good stuff—when he wasn't figuring out how to get them. I picture Herman always on the make. When he was feeling particularly satisfied with his life, which he did more and more the last few years, he would get a thoughtful expression on his face and say, "It's funny, isn't it, what motivates a kid. My parents never talked to me about college. They didn't give a damn if I went or not but they paid the bill." He always thought I made too much of a production of taking and picking up the boys, at boarding school or college—station wagon filled with squash racquets and stereo. He was right.

"Hell," he said, "I just threw a few things in a bag, said 'Goodbye,' and hitchhiked to college. It wouldn't have occurred to anyone to take me, and it wouldn't have occurred to me to expect it. They didn't even come to my graduation." There was a funny mixture of love, resentment at what had been missing, and pride that he "did it anyway." I know that after he established a successful practice nothing would have made him happier than to do things for his father, but by then his father had died.

It *is* funny what motivates a kid. Hy grew up in a cultural Sahara. He was the only one in his immediate family who went to college. He never mentioned a home that had books or music in it, but he tried to teach himself to understand and appreciate culture in all its forms. He had an extensive record collection of symphonies, some with the seals still unbroken. He would sit himself down sometimes, like an earnest schoolboy and listen purposefully, trying to like it.

But he never did. Later he repeated the lessons on tape, but with no more success. He was very sensitive to some art forms, especially Oriental art. We spent an unplanned and hurried day in Bangkok once and arrived at Jim Thompson's beautiful house on the Klong just at closing time. A kindhearted guide let us wander through by ourselves for an hour. Hy was almost reverential in his appreciation of some of the Buddhas. We both loved stopping at Mona Kaia on our way home from a trip partly because of the beautiful Oriental art that is there. We especially loved the large Buddha that sat at the top of the stairs leading to our room.

Music in any form was not particularly Hy's thing. He never recognized any of the big band songs when I'd say, "Oh, gee. Remember that one?" And he didn't remember ever having danced to one of them—which made me realize he was working hard, getting started, and cutting fiscal corners during those pre-war dancing years. He did a lot of dancing later on—even took dancing lessons—but that isn't the same.

His growing up was not family fun and games. He often mentioned that his family never celebrated birthdays—never even acknowledged them. Imagine, no paper hats or snappers that you pulled on, that made a noise and told your fortune. I didn't really believe him until we went to dinner at his sister Billie's house on his sixtieth birthday. I thought it was going to be a party, but I was the only one there who knew it was his birthday.

His attitude toward his mother was a little like Portnoy's: loyalty, and a grudging respect because she

102

was his mother. He heard me admonishing one of my sons to clean his plate once and said, "Oh, God, leave him alone. My mother said it to me so often I still eat stuff I don't want."

He was on a year's fellowship abroad, having just graduated with honors from the University of Syracuse Medical School when his father died at age fifty-four. Hy finished out what was a broadening and unforgettable experience for him in Europe, still not knowing. When he returned he found his mother a widow with a $5,000 life insurance policy and nothing else. She gave him most of the $5,000 to set himself up in practice, and he supported her for the next forty years, in a manner to which a good Jewish mama soon grew accustomed. He made a deal with his sister Billie, "You listen to her, and I'll pay the bills." It worked out satisfactorily for all. Hy visited his mother often, but they were quick stops—five minutes to say hello and see that she had whatever she needed.

He never suggested to me that she had been in any way a burden to him or that he resented all those years of running two households. He showed his hand only once, when I made a facetious remark about my son David being "the crutch of my old age." He stopped me short and his voice was stern, "Don't ever say a thing like that again. It's a damn poor joke. It's no joke at all." It fascinated me that she never worked in all those years, or apparently even considered it.

I met Mrs. Tarnower only once. She was blind by then and came with her sister for sunning and swimming while I was visiting Hy. The family talk at that time was "I guess they're going to get married." I was wearing the beautiful ring Hy had given me. Her sister said, "It's Mrs. Harris, she's very pretty." "Harris. Harris?" Momma asked. "Is that the Jewish Harrises?" Never mind what she looks like, let's make sure she isn't goyim! Hy always found that an amusing story.

Hy had mixed feelings about being a Jew. One moment he resented it and thought of it as an infirmity, the next moment he was reading another book about where the ancient Hebrew tribes came from, and who they really were. "You know," he said to me one evening in a particularly expansive mood, "I'm an agnostic. Now if you were an agnostic, you'd just be an agnostic. But I'm a Jewish agnostic. You never stop being Jewish." And then, as though he had exposed too much, he laughed and said, "What the hell. If I hadn't been Jewish it would have been too easy!" I loved that line.

Socially, and perhaps even intellectually, Hy might have preferred the upper middle-class wealthy Wasps of Scarsdale to the rich, rich, rich Jews of Manhattan, but it wasn't an option he ever really had. It wasn't until the late 1970s that he was asked to be a member of the Westchester Country Club.

"*Now* they ask me," he said, with a rueful smile and some honest bitterness in his voice. "It would have meant so much to me to be asked thirty years ago. What do I want with the Westchester Country Club today? I was the personal physician of four presidents of that club, but not good enough to be a member." I remember touching his arm and saying, "Herm, when you told them 'no thank you' I hope you were polite."

Every spring some of Hy's old Wasp friends and patients in Scarsdale gave a series of lovely dinners, and parties, usually crowded around Memorial Day weekend. Hy and I went to them together and enjoyed them for fourteen years. He was proud to be invited because, as he put it, "I think I'm the only Jew they ask." (Actually, there were one or two others.) They were the comfortably wealthy, old shoe type of people I had grown up with, not the rich, rich, rich, and of Hy's friends, certainly the ones I started out feeling most at home with. They were also the ones who liked me least.

The anti-Semitism I had lived with so long in Grosse Pointe, Michigan, was present at those parties but they were genuinely fond of Hy, and I never really thought about the other until one of them said after Hy was dead, "Oh yes. We often went to Hy's to dinner. The food and wine were beautiful, but he always invited us with Jews." Since Hy was a Jew, and his family was Jewish, and most of his friends were Jews, it stood to reason one would rub elbows with them at his home. The only "goyim" things about Hy were "those Scarsdale parties" each spring, and the women he slept with. As for the latter, maybe that was happenstance—or personal preference; or maybe it was Herman's way of saying, "Screw the Gentiles."

I know that for me those years of loving Hy were a lesson in anti-Semitism, something that is still rampant in our country today. And so much of it came from the mouths of decent people who simply don't hear themselves, and who would be genuinely upset if you pointed it out to them. "We looked at a new house in Darien, Jean. You should have seen the bathrooms—hideous pink—so Jewish looking." "His wife is pretty nice, but her hair—terribly Jewish looking." I'm glad I was brought up by a mother who was incapable of bigotry in any of its forms.

If there was any in me it didn't last very long. I know I was anxious that Hy not wear a particular blue and beige and brown summer jacket of his when he met some of my Grosse Pointe friends for the first time. But that was because I knew how establishment we all were and I didn't want anything to get in the way of their seeing what an interesting man he was. A few months later I loved him so completely it didn't matter to me what he wore or what anyone else might think of him. I wanted people to like him but if they didn't it didn't change anything for me.

Mr. and Mrs. Tarnower came from Poland. Hy was unsure about the family's true origin. We went to Poland together in 1976. He wanted to visit the ghetto in Warsaw, and the basement of the Gestapo Headquarters that is now a shrine to the countless Jews who died there. It was very important to him to go, but having seen it he said little and didn't seem deeply moved. But by then he worked at not being deeply moved, or not appearing to be. At first he said the family had probably come from the Polish town of Tarnow—sounds reasonable. But later, in Bulgaria, we met a woman who said there was a small town not far from where she had grown up with a name that sounded like Tarnow too. She wrote the name of the town on a match clip I still have.

What makes you keep things like that—and why does it still matter to me where they came from? Until we left Bulgaria, Hy spent an inordinate amount of time studying Bulgarian faces. He decided his nose and his father's nose were "definitely Bulgarian." I loved Hy's face, his beautiful dark brown eyes and what I thought was a fascinating profile. It reminded me of some of the Egyptian heads at the Metropolitan and I used to tease him, "I will always believe there was a little hanky panky at the palace, Herm before Moses got the family out of town." I think he rather liked the idea.

Hy went through college and medical school in fou

years. I imagine he was a very cocky young man. He looked like one in a college picture that I saw—with a great shock of hair he was hardly recognizable. A man who had known him during his college years introduced himself to me during the trial. I asked what he was like then. He smiled and said, "Full of hell!"

Hy told me, a number of times, that he never took notes in class, and was inclined to look out the window during lectures. It didn't mean he wasn't listening though, so if the professor commented on what looked like inattentiveness he could always repeat what had been said. He did the same thing in the army—which, with his hat pushed back, and his cocky manner, must have annoyed more than one superior officer.

I was one of those earnest characters who wrote down every word—and then underlined it in red, and studied the notes assiduously.

We both had taken history courses from Professor Hans Kohn, I at Smith, Hy later as an adult at New York University. He was a brilliant lecturer, and he and Hy became friends. Hy's fertile brain required an occasional evening with the Kafka and casserole set, although over the long haul, to be with "the right people" he could endure mind-bending boredom.

The Kohns and Hy and I spent an interesting weekend together in Purchase years ago. Hans was not happy with quite so much conspicuous consumption, but he did enjoy Hy's gift for asking good questions and being a good listener.

I read in a newspaper description of Hy that he never listened, just talked. Quite the contrary. Until the last few years, he listened much, much more than he talked—socially at least. I can't speak for the office. He may have acquired the habit at Syracuse where he was kidded about his "Brooklyn accent," and was called "Brooklyn" for the first year he was there. Freshman year, with characteristic Tarnower grit and determination, he took a speech course and began practicing in front of the mirror.

Slowly the sounds that screamed "Brooklyn" began to recede. He worked at it for four years. Henry Higgins might have spotted the vestiges of those sounds thirty-five years later when I met him, but I didn't. It was a "Tarnower" accent by then, obviously New York, but all the r's were in the right places, and the general effect was pleasant as far as I was concerned. The last six or seven years he began saying "vawze" instead of "vase," which seemed a little more gilding than the lily needed, but if that was self-improvement, too, so be it.

Hy learned to dance, to play golf, to play tennis, to shoot, to cast for salmon the same way—practice, practice, practice.

He could lose gracefully, at least to all outward and visible signs, but all his life he played everything to win. He would never start a golf match without at least a half-hour's warm-up on the practice tee. I have seen him practice casting for four hours nonstop, in the rain, and then after lunch and a nap give it a go for four hours more. He would watch a gin game or a bridge game, observing "tactics" as he called them, and find a significant lesson in something that had no meaning to me at all.

If he were going to do something he worked very hard to do it well. And he worked hardest at being a good doctor. He enjoyed his years at Syracuse and kept in close touch with classmates all over the country, and all over the world. He even went back to his forty-fifth reunion, which didn't seem like something he would do. We visited one of his classmates in

Teheran years ago. He was obstetrician to the Empress by then, and had delivered that much wanted heir to the Peacock Throne.

The year after medical school, Hy won a scholarship abroad and while he traveled and studied he made other lifetime friends; very special ones were a young Dutch doctor and his wife, who over the years were to have nine children, and six of them became doctors too. They visited often on Purchase Street. Hy's fellowship grant was for $1,500, a large amount in the early 1930s. It was to cover all travel and living expenses. He studied part of the year in England and then moved over to Paris. He showed me the house on the Left Bank where he lived for five months in an attic room.

"You could see the river if you leaned way out the window!" It was there in Paris that he saw his first pink chestnut tree, and decided on the spot to have his own some day. He had several of them there in Purchase, and he welcomed their blossoms each spring with great pleasure and always remembered again that spring in Paris. Hy's gift for appreciation of the things he liked and understood was boundless. It gave me vicarious pleasure just watching him enjoy—breathing deep and smelling the viburnum on a summer night, looking out over the pond he had built, listening to the ridiculous sound of the frogs at night, checking to see how the two small tulip trees were, "volunteers" that had suddenly appeared at the end of the driveway.

Hy took his internship at Bellevue. He was proud of having served there. We drove by from time to time and he always pointed out the old red building where interns slept—when they had a few minutes—which wasn't often. It usually reminded him that later the club for doctors who had served their internship at

Bellevue was closed to him because he was a Jew. I can't believe that it's still true—hard to believe that it was then, but he went to a meeting once, assuming he was a member, and was told he wasn't, and couldn't be. As for cardiology, it wasn't a particular choice of his. It was hardly a field of practice then, "so they opened it to a Jew!" He went on to take his boards in internal medicine as well, and then, though cardiology was always his special field, he really practiced as a general practitioner for the next forty years—"just a country doctor" he liked to say, with something less than a modest smile.

His years at Bellevue, and maybe the growing-up process in Brooklyn as well, convinced him early on that he wanted no part of New York City practice. While riding the ambulance, picking up kids who'd been bitten by rats, Bowery drunks mutilated in accidents, people hurt who would be mended only to go back and be hurt the same way again, he told himself he wanted to go where he could make more of a difference. And anyway, always the pragmatist, he wanted no long lines of traffic to get to the office and home again. He lived his life right from the start in a way to gladden the heart of Adam Smith—or Ayn Rand. Enlightened self-interest illuminated the path. He was never a do-gooder—but he did a lot of good. Not I. I was born to be Don Quixote, never consciously looking for windmills, but constantly finding them. I don't know whether it was being a teacher or a rather complex woman that made it inevitable.

It took Hy two years to find a suitable place in Scarsdale to live and to work. Same old problem. He was Jewish. Then, finally, having settled into an apartment where he could both live and work, he waited for patients. "I didn't go to a movie for years for fear a patient would call while I was out." I can hear him saying it. "I went to the synagogue one day, thinking that I could meet people that way. But when I got there I felt guilty about using it when I didn't believe what it taught—so I left. I've always been embarrassed that I did it."

He took on all comers, and since it was the depression there were some who couldn't pay. Not to worry. There was Tony who brought fresh flowers and vegetables to Hy's house every Thursday until the day Hy died, in gratitude for all the doctoring he had done for Tony and his large family all through the depression and right up to the time he went off to war. There was Joe who would stop work on anyone else's car to fix Hy's because Hy had cared for Joe and his family through some hard years. There were Margaret and Willy and Tubby and others.

Hy never talked about them, but over the years it was hard to miss how many there were. It made me very proud of him. His house, and later his wine cellar, was filled with gifts from grateful patients—an eclectic collection at best, but obvious expressions of gratitude and affection. The "valuable art collection" the papers talked about at his death was largely a collection of "loving hands at home," therapy paintings that nobody but Hy would have hung. The paintings he had bought himself were in the $100-$200 range—a wax resist from Kenya—a delightful watercolor called "The Gamblers" from Yugoslavia.

His Buddhas, large and small, some handsome bronzes, and the stone carving over his mantle were the closest Hy himself came to buying "art." He loved the ostrich egg he found in Tanzania. He loved the anka he bought for $10 from the elephant driver in Nepal, and his favorite piece was simply a small rock he picked up on the island of Cos, where Hippocrates had taught. He kept it on his dresser with a small ivory figure sitting on it.

3.

By the time World War II came Hy had a fine practice established, and had invested heavily in expensive equipment for his office. As a bachelor he knew he would be gone "for the duration," and as a man who was always thinking ahead, he knew there would be a doctor shortage back home. He looked around for a good doctor with wife and kids and a high draft number, and made a deal.

If the doctor would move into Hy's office, and keep the expensive equipment paying for itself, he would guarantee the doctor $500 per month. That was a lot of money in 1941, more than the young doctor had made, and Hy was prepared to pay the difference out of his army pay if the practice didn't live up to his expectations. The deal was made and both doctors prospered. I guess in a way this was the beginning of the Scarsdale Medical Group. The young man who held down the medical home front for four years has just recently retired from the group.

Hy thrived playing his role in the war. He became a colonel and enjoyed the privileges of rank for the first time in his life. True to army tradition for snafus, though he was a cardiologist and internist his longest tour of duty was in a psychiatric hospital. It must have been a rather trying time for everyone because Hy had almost no use or respect for psychiatry. He used to say, "There are exactly three psychiatrists in the City of New York I'd send a patient to. The rest aren't worth a damn." The hospital was in Kentucky, and Hy used what time off he could wangle to hunt, birds and broads. He became very good at both.

When he finally knew he was going overseas, his last worldly act was to race out and buy a portable deck chair. He enjoyed crossing the Pacific much more than those who sat on the hard deck and leaned against smoke stacks. That chair became rather famous during the crossing and was probably won and lost in a number of poker games. I would be very surprised if Old Herm didn't finally sell it at a profit.

The high point of his army career was being chosen a member of the Atomic Bomb Commission to go into Nagasaki on the first plane to enter the city after the dropping of "the bomb." He was proud that he had been chosen for the mission, and for the little piece of history that it made of him, but he never talked about what it was like or how he had felt walking through the devastation and horror. I asked him direct questions about it a number of times but the answers invariably cut off the next question. He lectured at Williams College directly after the war, but after that he had little or nothing to say about it.

A year and a half before the war was over, feeling his usual far-sighted and optimistic self, Hy wrote his sister Billie and asked her to order him a Cadillac "with everything on it." He didn't want "everything on it" but he figured that kind of an order wouldn't be lost or put on the bottom of the pile. Obviously there would be a long waiting line for cars when the war ended, and he wanted to be at the head of it. A doctor needs a car. Billie didn't put in the order and Hy never completely forgave her. I must have heard about that unordered Cadillac at least a dozen times. And it was thirty-five years later!

He was like an elephant when it came to things you had done to displease him. He brought them up repeatedly. It always surprised me that he did. At the risk of sounding sexist I think of it as a female

113

characteristic. I finally said to him when he was bemoaning one of my old transgressions, "Hy, that was eight years ago! If my sins are so few that you have to dredge them up from eight years ago, I think I have a pretty good track record. From now on let's make anything older than a year off limits." He laughed and said he would, but he didn't remember.

His first few months back in Scarsdale after four years away at war taught him a lesson that changed his life-style for the rest of his life. "I had glued myself to the office for years for fear I'd lose patients if I weren't always there. Then I took four years off and nobody seemed to know I'd been gone. I figured what the hell was all the sitting home for. From then on, when I wanted to take a two, or four, or six week vacation, I took it. It never affected my practice."

In the years right after the war he moved several times, always expanding his office. When he moved into a new private apartment his first worldly act was to have the gas disconnected so that none of the women in his life would insist on cooking for him, and fixing little intimate dinners at home. For more than *twelve* years he ate every meal out, breakfast, lunch, and dinner. No wonder he enjoyed dinner at home so much, after he had bought a house, and Henri and Suzanne had taken up residence with him.

Hy drove around Westchester for years looking for a piece of property "with a view." When he discovered the Pforzheimer property he loved it at once. He spent hours sitting on the old brick wall to the left of the deck he built—looking out at Long Island Sound in the distance. It was several years before he persuaded the family to sell him a little over five acres with the pool, the pool house, and the tennis court.

The pool house consisted of a large living room, dining room with an old stone fireplace at one end, a

114

tiny kitchen, two dressing rooms and baths, and a terrace room between—also with a large open fireplace. Hy added a large living room to the right of the pool house, with a bedroom, dressing room, and two baths above, and a garage down below. A swamp area he turned into a lovely pond with an island in the middle. He never stopped planting perennials around it and it grew lovelier every spring. Later, after I knew him, and he had asked me to marry him he added two bedrooms and two baths on the other side of the house. I didn't know until years later that while I was picturing where the children's books and toys would go, the carpeting, draperies, and bedspreads, all very good goods were a gift from his last paramour. She was then married to someone else, but Herman never looked a gift horse in the mouth. Gold watches, gold cuff links, gold fountain pens, gold tie pins, gold belt buckles, needlepointed vests and slippers. It was quite a collection.

I said to him the first year we met, "Someday, Herman, if I'm ever very rich, I'm going to buy you a Steuben hunting bowl and collect all the dates so lovingly inscribed, engraved, needlepointed, and hemstitched all over this house—and have them all etched on the bowl . . . the true Tarnower hunting trophy—certainly better than those elephant tusks. And who knows, Herm, if you give it your best shot you may be able to fill the whole damned calendar."

It amazes me as I reread that that I could have said anything that callous without really knowing what I was saying—or to whom I was saying it. Too much of it was like a play. I made fun of the truth instead of facing it. Hy told me all of the gifts came from "grateful patients." It was years before that term had a pejorative ring to it for me. I simply never put two and two together. Not even one and one. That "grateful patient" was Hy's euphemism for the newest woman in his life simply didn't occur to me. When a new pair of gold cuff links appeared on the dresser they were always from a "grateful patient."

I'm afraid Herman left a number of grateful patients around Westchester who didn't get the treatment at the office. And they weren't exclusively in Westchester either. He met a woman on the long flight to Kenya once, the wife of a prominent American. By the time I met him in Kenya a week later she was already a "grateful patient." She didn't even know his right name. The note slipped under our bedroom door was addressed to Dr. Hyman Tarnower. He had a rather sticky two or three days explaining all the phone calls to the room, and why he had to keep running downstairs to "check reservations" and "check traveler's checks." And I didn't suspect a thing because I didn't want to and I didn't want others to. It seems to me an unnatural, cynical, most unloving way to live. But Hy loved his life and I didn't love mine, so what does it all mean? What is the code?

I hasten to add that Hy gave most generously too, often more generously than he received. He loved buying cases of champagne for special friends, invariably those who already had a cellar full of it. He was quicker than anyone at any table to pick up the check, and he certainly returned in kind the favor of all those golden baubles. The last thing he wanted was to be beholden to anyone. It made him feel vulnerable. Unfortunately, the deep sentiment with which many gifts were given to him he soon forgot. Just before Hy died, my son Jim lost the watch that his father had left to him. He immediately volunteered to give him a very grand gold watch to replace it. When I recognized it as one a woman had given

116

him I told him he really ought to be ashamed, and wouldn't let Jim have it.

There seemed to be different levels of giving for Hy, not necessarily classified by cost so much as by caring. We were waiting in the airport in Denpasar at the end of a trip to Bali one day, I reading, Hy looking in the little airport shops. Suddenly an attractive woman sitting near me turned to her husband and said, "My God, did you see that man over there? He's buying jewelry as though it were prizes for popcorn boxes!" It was Herman, filling up the General Fund. He did the same in Ceylon, and in one of the bazaars in Khartoum. I've seen some gold earrings and a large topaz ring I watched him point out in Colombo, Ceylon, being worn by one of his "grateful patients" in Scarsdale.

Years ago, when he went to China he asked, "What do you want me to bring you?" I said, "Anything at all Hy, but please just buy one." Later, before he handed me a very beautiful jade ring I said, "Hy, whatever it is, please keep it if you bought it by the pound." He said, "Dammit, this was expensive. I couldn't have bought more than one." He saw me wearing a pair of costume earrings I had bought at Saks once, and said, "Where did you get those? I'm supposed to buy your earrings." Over the years he gave me some handsome pieces of gold jewelry, most of it, I'm happy to say, bought thoughtfully, and lovingly for me. Some of it came from the General Fund.

Hy's timing, when he bought his house and the clinic, was fortuitous to say the least. The price was right and both of them gave him many years of pleasure and deep personal satisfaction. The city of Scarsdale was not especially happy to have a clinic built right in the middle of a very posh suburban area, but it was tastefully done, quite unobtrusive, and over the years has proved a great asset and convenience to the community. Every step of the planning and building entailed a fight, council meetings, irate property owners of Heathcote, articles in the Scarsdale papers—the whole bit. It took vision, determination, courage, and a very thick skin to see the thing through to completion.

Hy had them all. He was sure all the fuss was just another manifestation of "the Jewish thing" but it probably wasn't. He was trying to get more parking space for the clinic when I came into the picture. He had the acreage but the community didn't want to run the risk of "more traffic." He regaled me with stories of the fight and I pictured myself, little Wasp wife, dressed in my most respectable suburban costume, standing beside my man in battle. Unfortunately—or fortunately perhaps—it wasn't to be. Hy wouldn't let me go with him to any council meetings. They finally compromised and some of the land was made parking space and some of the land was left park.

The house gave him as much pleasure as the clinic gave him satisfaction. It was a bright, cool, open house, with lovely large rooms except for the kitchen. That remained butler pantry size in spite of the glamourous meals that were constantly being prepared in it. There was never a woman in the house whose opinion and convenience were a priority item—not even Suzanne, the cook, though she probably came closer to it than any other woman.

Dinner at Hy's was very fancy—and grew fancier as his celebrity grew. He had learned about wines from Alfred Knopf, a true oenophile. Alfred and Blanche Knopf, and Hy and heaven knows who, drove through the French wine country together more than twenty years ago. During that trip Hy ordered many cases of wine shipped to him, most of them recommended by Alfred, and that began his wine cellar.

By the time he died, his wine was probably the most valuable thing he owned. He was a generous host, and he loved giving small dinner parties of six or eight. Like Melville he knew "Who has but once dined his friends has tasted whatever it is to be Caesar." I think he felt a little like Caesar at the head of the table.

Suzanne did him proud every time. Game birds and chicken were most often the main dish. He loved the "Oohs" and "Aahs." He loved someone trying to guess the vintage of the wine. And he loved good conversation. He was very conscious of the interests and talents of a particular guest, and always threw out a few provocative questions, and then sat back and enjoyed the answers—that is, after he had asked every man in the room, "Are you buying or selling?"

Hy's love of good conversation and his earnest efforts to encourage such conversation, sometimes against mighty odds, were one of his outstanding qualities. He hungered to learn and to know. He had great respect for the expertise of others. And it drove him wild to have to sit and listen to somebody's small talk when something of interest was being said on the other side of the table. He kept his dinner parties small and then tried gamely to have one conversation at a time. If someone in the room, or at the table, started a second conversation he was quite uninhibited about saying in a very authoritative way, "Let's have just one conversation going at a time."

An old friend of ours was reminiscing with me about Hy recently and remembered the time he was sitting at her dinner table. She turned to say something to him and he shushed her with the "just one conversation" line. When he suddenly remembered it was her house he added, "Please." Some people resented this in Hy. Others made fun of it. I found it an imminently logical and acceptable modus operandi. If you stop to notice at your next party you will probably find that almost everyone is talking and almost no one is listening. In many ways Hy was a very civilized man, and more sensitive than many supposed. He said to me one night, after the guests had gone, and almost like a hurt child, "Have you ever noticed I'm always asking other people what they think, but they never ask me what I think?"

What he had as a conversationalist he lacked as an interior decorator. I didn't like any of the furniture in Hy's house, or what passed for decorating. On my shoestring budget I thought I did much better. But somehow that didn't matter. It would never have occurred to me to try to redecorate. Early and late Second Avenue "antique" shop or early and late bachelor was the general period and style—but there were always fresh flowers and somehow the total effect was generally pleasant and bright.

The living room was getting very crowded—nothing was removed as stuff was added. Where there should have been leather Hy settled for plastic. The webbing in the bamboo chairs was perilously thin, and once, nicely aged wrought iron pieces were painted shiny black by Mrs. Tryforos when Hy and I were away on a trip. Does anyone find that bizarre besides me?

I liked the way the house was only because it satisfied Hy. Every piece of furniture, every piece of bric-a-brac had a story to it, a small piece of his life. That was good enough for me. Far more open and honest than a nifty packaged deal from an interior decorator whom he could easily have afforded. Each time I bought something for the house, and that was almost constantly, it was done in an effort to improve slightly while maintaining the status quo—to keep it the way he liked it, but keep it fresh.

The only time the rugs and carpets were cleaned in fourteen years I paid the bill. When a lamp shade fell apart I replaced it. When a chair needed reupholstering or recaning, I had it done. Many things Hy didn't even know had been done, and I didn't stand around saying, "What a good girl am I!" New living room curtains, water glasses, dishes, sheets, towels, irons, all the unsexy stuff you couldn't have engraved were my domain. And that's the way I wanted it.

Hy often said to me, "I've never asked anything of you," and since it seemed to make him happy to believe it, I spent fourteen years letting him believe it. He never understood that the hardest thing he could ask of me was "nothing." There were nights on trips when I waited until he was asleep to wash one of those three pairs of tired khakis he traveled with for fourteen years. He always insisted that he didn't want me to "bother" and sooner or later in our wanderings through Asia and Africa we'd reach a place with room service. I didn't want him ever to feel "obligated." I didn't want to be part of "the cuff link collection" either—and I never was.

Scarsdale:
The Diet

The story of Hy's book is a chapter in itself. It was a watershed in his life, and nothing, most of all Hy, was ever quite the same again. I was in Virginia by then but each trip back was less the same, and each trip back made me happy to see him someplace besides home—Palm Beach, Nassau, Washington— somewhere that the change wasn't so stark. Suzanne said it to me one day. "It isn't the same here now. There's a bad feeling. I don't know what it is. It isn't the same."

Hy was becoming a little like a child who's been struggling to win the game, "Mother, May I?" and suddenly and deliberately took a giant step backward. Demur if you wish, and tell me I am still impressed by a curtsy, but I found something sad about a man who had stood in front of a mirror at Syracuse University for four years practicing diction ending up with an entourage of hangers-on, and a woman who called him "Ma Chair" and "Super Doctor."

What was the whole exercise for—to get so rich you could revert to type? And all the time I had filed i under "c" for "character" and "w" for wonderful He stopped being that marvelous, bright man getting "ahead" by some reasonably acceptable set of rules. He had always made some of his own rules, but now he could write them all. Wherever he was standing was the head of the line, so screw saying, "May I?"

Hy's book made him rich (richer) and famous, and those are things I'm sure were fun to be. Imagine trying to save a man from all that. Imagine believing he was too good for it. I did everything I could to persuade Hy from writing the book, but when the contract was signed and there was no turning back I did everything I could to help make it a little better than it otherwise would have been.

We were sitting in the living room on Purchase Street one Sunday in April 1978, *The New York Times* spread around us as usual, when someone called Hy and said, "Say, you're famous! There's a mention of your diet in the *Times Sunday Magazine*." We quickly turned to the right page, and sure enough, in an article about diets, Hy's was mentioned. We both thought that was quite exciting. Diet had always played a key role in Hy's ministering to the sick, especially his heart patients.

He had said, "No fatty meats, no butter, no bread, no liquor, no rich desserts" so many times he finally sat in his office one morning, wrote out what he considered a sensible diet, the diet he essentially followed most of his adult life, and had his secretary type it up and run it off on the mimeo machine. It took him "about an hour." He gave out those mimeographed sheets for nineteen years before the book was born.

Many of his patients were the well-heeled and well-traveled and they took the diet with them all over the country and all over the world. As word of it spread— or as Samm Sinclair Baker put it, "As word of mouth expanded," there were so many demands for it that

123

Hy's mailing costs finally hit more than two thousand dollars a year. Some people sent self-addressed envelopes but most of the expense Hy paid out of his own pocket. He didn't know it at the time but he was casting bread upon the waters, and those sheets were making his book famous before it was even written. Seymour Topping, managing editor of *The New York Times*, was an old friend of Hy's, knew of the diet, and I think it was he who started the ball rolling.

By early that Sunday afternoon Oscar Dystel, an acquaintance of Hy's and then head of Bantam Books, had called to see if Hy was interested in writing a book. By that evening three other publishers had called. Each time Hy came away from the phone laughing and shaking his head, saying, "This is silly as hell. How could you make a book out of a one page diet?" A week or so later so many people had approached him on the subject of a book he was having second thoughts. Maybe he would combine the diet with some good common sense observations and medical practices that forty years of experience had proven sound and valuable. He had some things worth saying. Maybe this was the time.

He made a brief outline of what might conceivably be included in such a book, and took the outline to his old friend Alfred Knopf for advice. Alfred simply wouldn't give the subject the time of day, and kept turning the conversation to things of greater interest to him. Helen, Alfred's second wife, was kind and encouraging right from the start, but Alfred gave him nothing. Hy was deeply hurt by this and never really forgave Alfred. "I've spent a lot of hours ministering to that man, going to him at all hours of the day and night, listening to his problems and he wouldn't give me ten minutes of his time." I knew just how he felt that Monday night in March.

Hy thought that Alfred could at least have told him more about Samm Sinclair Baker, and advised him about contracts. In all fairness to Alfred, maybe he felt as others of us did who loved Hy, that a diet book would not reflect well on him, and he shouldn't go ahead with it. After the book was finally out Alfred praised it highly. I'm afraid I was never courteous enough to do the same.

Hy's next approach was to Random House through Tony Schulte. Tony is Arthur's son, an old friend of Hy's, and an executive at Random House. Like Alfred, Tony thought Hy's outline was thin. Tony's step-mother, Vivian, thought Hy was in way over his head since nutrition was certainly not his field, and Tony wrote what I thought was a decent letter saying in the nicest possible way for Hy to think about it some more before he went ahead with the book.

It impressed me as a letter that Tony had spent a good deal of time composing. Hy was angry when he showed it to me. He never asked favors, never. Now, for the first time in those two close relationships he was asking for something and he didn't get it. Or he didn't get it in the form he wanted it. He didn't want them to publish a book for him, but he did want their expertise on how to go about it.

My feeling was that Tony was putting friendship ahead of making an easy buck, but maybe I'm wrong. Certainly Hy didn't see it that way and he plunged ahead completely on his own. If his friends weren't going to help him there were plenty of people around who would, hucksters who knew that the timing was right and the advance publicity was red hot.

Samm Sinclair Baker, who had co-authored *Dr. Stillman's Fourteen Day Weight Loss Program*, called and said he would be happy to write the book, and in a short time he had a contract and 50 percent of all monies. Later, when Hy began to realize how much that 50 percent was going to be, and how little he thought of Samm's writing, it gnawed at him. But he always said, "Well, Samm thought of the title, which was very important, and I never could have written it without him, so I guess it wasn't a bad deal." Samm wrote him about writing another book together but Hy made it clear that if there were a second book it wouldn't be with Mr. Baker.

By August of 1978 Samm was busily grinding out chapters of the book and Suzanne van der Vreken was spending every spare moment at her typewriter doing the recipes. Mrs. Baker later changed some of them, but the lion's share of them were the work of Suzanne. Samm's contribution to the recipes were some catchy little names. "Breast of Chicken Herman" and "Spinach Delight A La Lynn." I said. "My God! You actually saw this ahead of time and let him print it?" Hy said, "Well, Samm thought it was cute." It's adorable! I had tried a little cuteness too but Samm red penciled it. We were working on the table of contents, and since the diet, which is why you buy the book, doesn't come until Chapter IV, I suggested as its title "Enough of This Lovemaking, Off with the Calories!" I guess Samm found it too risqué. But you can't beat "Breast of Chicken Herman" for cute.

I had planned all summer to spend the last two weeks of August and Labor Day with Hy. When I arrived he was in a state I had never seen him in before. Samm had written the first few chapters of the book and Hy thought they were awful. He had made his own efforts to edit them, changing a word here or a tense there, but he wasn't satisfied with that either. He was genuinely upset. "I've signed a contract to publish this damned thing and look at it! Jesus!"

It was something he couldn't walk away from. It was also the first time in all the years I had known him that I was conscious of his profanity. And it was the first time in all those years that he needed a kind of help I could try to give. I knew that I wasn't a writer, but I knew that I could improve upon what he had.

I sat down at the table just outside the kitchen and started crossing out and rewriting. I sat there working for two entire weeks, day and night. It was my summer vacation. One of those nights Hy took Lynne Tryforos to a dinner party that their dentist gave. I was served a quick hamburger by Henri and went back to writing the book.

Hy's concession to "good manners" was to be home by 9:30. It wasn't the first time he had done it. The first time I had been sad that he was capable of doing it. That night I was too caught up in the work on the book to be concerned one way or the other. Disillusion had already set in, but then love and friendship are for better or for worse. Aren't they?

Hy's spirits began to rise as changes in the book were made. We had many favorite lines from Samm's original version but our first favorite was in his question and answer chapter. "Q: I want to lose five pounds. How long should I stay on the diet? A: Stay on the diet just long enough to lose the five or six pounds." I found more knee-slappers than Hy did, and after two weeks of my caustic remarks I'm not sure whether he was more teed off at me or Samm.

The last day of my writing holiday was a lovely sunny Labor Day and we took a leisurely drive up to Greenwich. In the course of the drive I told Hy it had been one of my happiest holidays with him because for once I knew I had done something helpful for him when so often it had been the other way. I didn't mention that it was happy in spite of his flagrant extra-curricular activities. Suddenly he turned to me and said, "Look, I'm going to give you $2,000 because it's convenient for me this way—I don't have to tell you why—and maybe next year I'll give you $2,000 more, but that's at my discretion. I don't have to if I don't want to." So much for a loving gift.

I left the next morning and wrote him a rather anguished letter about his callousness, but I don't believe I ever mailed it. He called several times as though nothing had happened and mentioned that he was having "a helluva fight" with some of the doctors at the clinic who were now claiming part of the book's potential returns . . . which by then were looking sizable. He said, "I'll just stop practicing medicine for a year if I have to—or maybe I'll move the office to the house, but by God they're not going to take this book away from me."

A few days later I saw an article about the Scarsdale Diet in one of the newspapers they sell at the grocery store checkout counter. The headline of the story was: "The Magic and Mysterious Chemical Formula of the Scarsdale Diet." It worried me because there wasn't any "chemical formula" and I didn't want anyone to think Hy had claimed it. I wrote him:

September 10, 1978

Dear Hy,

I'm glad that E. Rawson is doing a good job for you. I know it's a great relief and helps alleviate some of the mounting pressures in your life. Certainly, they're only temporary ones, but obviously too they're pretty onerous at the moment.

I hope the "knock-down fight" you mentioned has helped clear the air. I really don't see how you can avoid taking some time off after the book comes out. The demands on your time will be tremendous, whatever your contract with Dystel says. You'll have a "public" then and the public is probably more of a demanding taskmaster than publishers are. It might be a very handy tax break to take the house off for a year as your place of business anyway. Even though you talked about it with a certain amount of equanimity I think it is really dreadful for any of the doctors to expect to be paid proceeds from the book. It seems to me they're the only real losers if you take a year off. I think it's more a matter of wanting to hurt you than wanting the money. You are widely respected and admired, Hy, but you don't always bring out the best in people, because, as you've been told before, I'm sure, you often hurt them deeply. The only time I even think of your money is when I want to match you—hurt for hurt—and I know there are some hard times to come with the doctors— maybe you read my letter and resented it—but Monday when you offered me $2,000 "because it's convenient for me this way—I don't have to tell you why—and next year maybe I'll give you $2,000 more—but that's at my discretion, I don't have to if I don't want to. I don't owe it to you," your voice sounded as though you were offering a little tip to a $2,000 whore. It was cold and utterly contemptuous.

I don't want a pound of flesh, Hy. I was quite happy to settle for "thank you" and I still am. If the book's successful I hope you may decide on another trip, somewhere, anywhere, together. If I were an acquisitive woman you may be sure

129

that at the age of 55 I wouldn't be in the position I'm in.

You have said to me a hundred times "I never ask anything of you . . . I never ask anything of anyone." But my dear it isn't true. For starters, you ask every woman to be as incapable of love as you are. That's like asking her to be a paramecium, or a woodcock, or some damn thing she isn't. I spent a good deal of time this summer thinking about the qualities a woman should have to survive in today's world—men and women as a matter of fact. Then I wondered how a woman like me, who lacks many of the qualities, could presume to teach them to the young. My opening address to the girls was on this subject, and I'm told it was a very good talk. In fact I've been asked to give it again in Richmond in Oct. and in Washington in Nov. What it lacks in brilliance it makes up for in "down-home" sincerity. There'll be violins in the background! At any rate, my dear, I wish I had been born a door-mat or a man, instead of the miserable half-breed I've turned out to be. I want very much to feel like your equal—but love is no equalizer.

One of the female characteristics they call the "Anointment Syndrome" at Wharton School of Business, Univ. of Pa., is still strong in me even though I can talk quite objectively about it in others. In her heart of hearts most women think that sooner or later hands will be placed gently on her head and a voice will say, "You have been a good girl. You have done what you were told and done it well, and now I am going to promote you"—or reward you—or whatever.

I guess on Monday, I was expecting anointment—not a tip—and my idea of anointment from you, my dear, is just a pleasant drive in the country. That's all I bargained for. That's all I wanted.

This crazy article that really prompted me to write at all upset me at first. I thought it might mean lawsuits, etc. But the more I think about it the more useful to you it seems to be. It is a classic example of how people misread, misquote, mix-up, cash-in-on, or just plain prostitute a reputable thing. The "chemistry" myth is abroad in the land whether you encourage it or not. As long as you cover it in the chapter of Questions and Answers, no one can lay it at your feet. The fact is people want it to be a chemical miracle and they're pretty well disposed to believe it no matter what you tell them. It will, I'm afraid, sell books without any push from you. There are big months ahead Hy—please know I'm in the cheering section—not lined up for a piece of the action.

Love,
Jean

A week or so after my letter Hy sent me a check for $4,000 and this note:

MEMO FROM HERMAN TARNOWER
Wednesday

Dear Jean,

For reasons that I cannot explain, it is imperative that I make all book disbursements at this time.

I am enclosing a check for $4,000 that I hope you will accept.

131

I told him that I wouldn't cash it. He interpreted this to mean, poor troubled man, that I might be holding out for more, and offered to double it again. I cashed the check for $4,000, and admitted to myself that Hy had become a different man than the one I had imagined him to be, or the one he had once been.

I still don't know what possessed Hy in the best of spirits to intrude on an otherwise beautiful afternoon drive to make his $2,000 offer, but in retrospect I think it was either because there were so many people hovering around the till, or because for the first time in all our years of friendship he wasn't the giver, he was the taker or receiver, and it wasn't a role he was comfortable with. He didn't want to beholden to anyone. He had long since entered his "I don't love anyone, I don't need anyone" period and he wanted to be sure that I didn't leave with any illusions of grandeur.

After Hy's death Samm Sinclair Baker did a great deal of talking to the press about Mrs. Harris having absolutely nothing to do with *The Complete Scarsdale Medical Diet*. One of Hy's old friends was quoted as saying, "Mrs. Harris's name in the book's dedication was gratuitous kindness on the doctor's part" part of "his letting her down easy." Another said, "Mrs. Harris was jealous of the doctor's book."

Gratuitous kindness to a woman was something Hy was never guilty of. The remarks were made by people who didn't know either of us well or anything about our relationship.

We were down in Lyford Cay in Nassau visiting the John Loebs, sitting in bed as a matter of fact, when Hy handed me the first copy of the book, with the

132

kind of expression on his face that David and Jimmy had when they gave me the bookends they had made in manual training. "Look at the acknowledgment," he said, beaming. It took a great deal of tongue biting to keep from saying "Oh, Hy. How could you?" There, at the top of a long list of women who had served him in various capacities while the magnum opus took shape were the words:

> We are grateful to Jean Harris for her splendid assistance in the research and writing of this book.

There had never been anything that public about my friendship with Hy and I certainly didn't want it now. And the word "research" troubled me. My "research" had consisted of spending an hour in the White Plains Hospital library looking up definitions of "ketosis." I had more than enough of my own "research" to do and I certainly wouldn't have presumed to do it for a doctor. As for whether I did an appreciable amount of writing for the book, I did, and a number of people, including Henri and Suzanne van der Vreken, Samm Baker and Lynne Tryforos are quite aware of the fact.

Henri and Suzanne watched me writing, and rewriting for those two weeks, told me where to go in Rye to get Xerox copies made, saw the crumpled sheets of paper accumulate around me and heard the occasional obscenities as I exploded, "How in the hell did a man with his brains get involved in this creepy thing?" I went with Hy to deliver some of the rewrites to Samm's house, and by then Samm was getting a little testy about all the changes, and Hy was trying to be diplomatic but firm. Hy said himself, on a number of occasions, "Jean wrote the book." He said it to a woman who interviewed him for *The Washington Star* and I protested and walked away for fear the "socialite headmistress of the Madeira School" might get some publicity she certainly didn't want.

Sitting in my lawyer's office today are the chapters of the book as Samm wrote them and my handwritten corrections and rewritings. It was a large piece of work lovingly done to the best of my ability because I never stopped wanting the world to know Hy was as good as I thought he was. I didn't want him to look like a second string "diet doc" when he was a first string cardiologist and internist.

Later, of the almost four hundred potential jurors that were questioned in the process of picking a jury for the case of the People of New York State vs. Jean Harris there were probably fewer than thirty who didn't refer to a splendid physician named Dr. Herman Tarnower as "that diet doc." Ironically enough it was Assistant District Attorney George Bolen who rose and requested that the judge himself stop using the term. Judge Legget answered, "That's the way he's known, and I'll use the term if I choose."

Philadelphia: Springside School

I was a teacher for thirty-six years. The last twelve of them I combined administration and teaching. I had thought at first I would write about them another time, and maybe never. It would be easier that way. There is so much, it's hard to know what to put in and what to leave out. But if it is beyond the ability of some of Hy's closest friends to imagine that anything could have troubled me that March night except one of the doctor's girlfriends, then how could a stranger know what filled my life, moved me, motivated me, frustrated and exhausted me? How could he know unless I told him, and how could I write about myself leaving anyone with the thought that my life was so empty it held nothing but Hy?

There's a good deal of folklore about "headmistresses," remembered with a mixture of fun, fondness, and fear by those of us who matriculated at their various seats of learning. The place you had to sit when you were called before her "presence" for corrective purposes had different names at different schools, but meant the same thing. At Miss Hall's School it was called "the little green chair." At Laurel it was "the bench." At Springside it was "Miss

Potter's hot seat."

There is still a hot seat in every headmistress's office, but today the headmistress is sitting in it. Today, before degrees from the proper halls of ivy, one would have to list as minimal requirements for a successful school head, the hide of an iguana, need for a maximum of four hours sleep per night, a law degree, and a wife. Just about anyone on the campus grounds, or anyone within earshot of the campus grounds, would be happy to tell you how to run the place. The constituency is much wider than the school's size would suggest, and since every private school worth its salt has an annual deficit to cover each year, one's main occupation is often raising money instead of raising the intellectual level of the young.

On the other hand, teaching in a private school can still be quite agreeable, especially if you have a sizable family trust fund to pay your bills. It's harder than it used to be, but it can still be enjoyable.

By and large, a teacher in a good private school enjoys the privilege of teaching—not collecting the milk money, filling things out in triplicate, or patrolling the halls, but teaching. The state governments are doing their best to change this and spread the misery around, but one still can teach in a private school, or "independent" school as they prefer to be called.

You also enjoy in these schools reasonably competent students, probably as well motivated to work as any group of people in our country. That could be damning them with faint praise, but newspapers do love to refer to private school students as "preppies," the consummate country club set, and the coddled rich, when the truth is, if everyone on the Detroit assembly lines had been putting in the hours of honest-to-God-hard-labor that the average Exeter, Madeira, Farmington, Andover student does there would be more Chevies and fewer Toyotas on American highways.

Best of all, a private school teacher has the intellectual freedom, given certain agreed upon goals, to achieve those goals in ways that make sense to her. She can use a new book, spend a little extra time giving a play one week and make up any lost time another week. I have been in public schools where posted in the front office is the *exact* page every third grade reading class is to be on for that day—an educational travesty that doesn't seem to embarrass the administrator who posts it.

For the privilege of enjoying these intellectual freedoms, however, private school teachers pay in cold, hard cash. There is a popular and comforting myth beloved by many private school parents that private school teachers teach "for the sheer joy of it"—so they go through their professional lives paying their students' tuitions, motivated by all that unbridled joy. That is an honest observation, not a complaint on my part, since as a parent I was the recipient of much private school generosity.

The median salary of private school teachers is anywhere from $3,000 to $10,000 less per year than that of the public school teacher around the corner. Most boarding schools make up the difference by providing campus homes and meals for the faculty, adding, of course, some of the necessary parental responsibilities in return.

Some of us weighed the intellectual pluses, and the very practical plus that to teach in a private school in most states you didn't have to be state certified, which required countless tedious hours of "education courses," and opted for a lower salary. Required standards of proficiency in order to teach are very

137

much needed, but, as presently written by some states, they permit seriously unqualified people to teach, and keep out others.

I was told when I looked into a public school teaching job in Michigan, "Lady, Albert Einstein couldn't teach physics in a Detroit school if he didn't have a certificate." I was told by an accrediting official in the state of Virginia, "I could cry when I read the ungrammatical letters we receive from English teachers asking to renew their certification." That doesn't mean that there aren't outstanding teachers and scholars in the public schools, but it means there is a sizable amount of deadwood too.

Today, scores of students who list teaching as a profession they aspire to when they take their SAT exams, now rank below those of students checking fourteen other listed professions. In other words, if you aren't much of a scholar today, you are more apt to go into teaching than into fourteen other fields.

I was fortunate enough to begin my teaching in a splendid country day school in Grosse Pointe, Michigan—now known as University-Liggett School. I taught there for nineteen years. Both of my sons started school there in three-year nursery school. Jimmy went through seventh grade, David through tenth, both tuition free, before we moved to Philadelphia. A small salary was of little concern to me and the teaching was pure pleasure. Today, fewer schools give this important plus because of IRS complications.

In spite of the fact that it sounds much more liberated and impressive to be a female doctor or lawyer, you can't beat the combination of a gratifying profession and the knowledge that your children won't find the key under the mat—and you can vacation together. It was a lovely luxury for all of us.

For those teachers who didn't have children there were no compensating salary increases, however, so I was one of the parents who enjoyed what I consider the only truly unforgivable thing about private schools. The faculty pays a large slice of the tuition. The answer certainly doesn't lie in unionizing—that would close most private schools. It lies in educating alumnae and businesses to a better understanding of what a well-educated citizenry is worth.

I enjoyed the experience of teaching. My first two years of teaching were in American history to the seniors, civics to the ninth grade, and current events to the seventh grade. I taught thirty-two classes per week and was paid $18,000 per year and could hardly believe my good fortune. The year was 1946, and there was a serious teacher shortage.

After two years of watching me work until long after midnight to prepare classes, my husband Jim made me resign. The school said, "Would you consider working half a day? We need a kindergarten teacher and the children go home at noon." For the next two years I was a kindergarten teacher. After David was born I stayed home for two years except for trouping in Junior League plays in the public schools. I played Pinocchio and a mean sister in Cinderella.

One August, when Jimmy, my younger son, was three months old, my old school called to say their first grade teacher had been in an accident and it might be a month before they could replace her. Would I fill in? "Well, I'm not sure—what do they do in first grade?" "They learn to read—you'll love it." I hurried to the library to take out every book on reading I could find—and eleven years later I was still teaching first grade, one of the most intellectually exciting jobs a teacher can have.

It pleased me to have the opportunity to help

children start really thinking long before I had. I had an inquiring mind in the classroom, but I was more concerned about "the right answer" than anyone with an original idea can afford to be. I always coughed up what the teacher wanted—a coward's way out—and I missed a lot along the way as a result.

As a teacher, I am happy to say, I never made the same mistake. Nothing delighted me more than an offbeat answer or even "the wrong answer" from a student with a thoughtful reason and the courage to defend his idea or maybe just a lovely sense of humor. I guess I say "his" because as I look back and remember some of those splendid wrong answers they usually came from a little boy. I learned as a first grade teacher that a really bright child will often miss "simple" questions on a standardized test because his fertile brain has taken the question a step beyond the adult who made up the question.

We spent a lot of time painting in my classroom. I tried to get little girls in clean white pinafores to use their arms and elbows and even their feet for the fingerpaints—not just the top of the pinkie. We spent a whole year trying to figure out what color water is, and the class collected a grand portfolio of pictures showing every possible color of the sea, from pure gold to jet black. A mother of one of my students wrote me in prison that the seascape her then six-year-old daughter painted that year is still framed and hanging in her dining room.

We came to terms with the fact that there isn't a big empty space between the sea and the sky, and flower stems don't always stand ramrod straight, and we drew flowers the way they probably look to a ladybug. We listened to the songs of whales; we learned some poems by e. e. cummings, and we wrote our own endings to the story of Stuart Little. In a ninth grade civics class we spent some time trying to rewrite the Constitution in our own words and discovered it would be pretty hard to improve on it. And I spent some uncomfortable moments with a family lawyer who was very angry because I had given him a C on the work he had done for his client's child. We tried to define "civilization" in an eighth grade class, and some first graders tried to figure out the difference between work and play, a job so complicated we never did agree on anything definitive.

My first graders wrote a lot of plays, taking as characters the dolls and puppets the children brought for show and tell—or the masks they made for Halloween, or the people they thought might gather in a certain place at a certain time. They would make up their list of characters, each would choose the person or creature he or she wanted to be. Then I'd say, "Okay. Your part in this play is as good as you make it. Figure out whom you want to talk to, what you want to say, and write it down." They knew their letters and the sounds they made, and they would set to with a will.

That night I would take all their writing home, spread it all over the living-room floor and begin to put the pieces together like the parts of a puzzle. Somehow, they always came together and became part of a logical whole. I always encouraged them to "write their own script," a privilege Hy would later remind me I didn't have.

"You can't write the script, Jean," he'd say. "You can't write the script."

My master's thesis was built around a history of Detroit which I wrote one year for a particularly bright group of six-year-olds: There were no holds barred on the vocabulary. I would write a chapter every week or two, read it to them, and within a day

141

or two if not on the spot, they could all read it too. They loved watching the book grow and taking it home to read something to the family that they knew had substance to it.

They became totally immersed in old Fort Pontchartrain, made a model of it in their spare time (it ended up on display in the Detroit Public Library), made visits to the Historical Society, on their own time, and by spring, when I had had more than my fill of Fort Pontchartrain, the children insisted upon writing a play about it, completely on their own. They started, as we always did, by listing who was probably there in the spring, what they might be doing, and then choosing their characters and writing the parts. While I have worked with every age group from nursery school to high school, I will always believe that teachers who have never worked with first graders have missed a special part of the joy of teaching and learning.

Why does a reasonably happy teacher become a school administrator? Very easy. She needs the money. Much as been written about Mrs. Harris's need for "power," "need to be in control," written by friend and foe alike, but the fact is even in 1966 it was rather difficult to support yourself and two children on $8,500 a year (before taxes!).

It is also true that while I like to talk about ideas I am an impatient person who likes to see the idea become a reality. I don't see myself "needing to be in control" but everyone else does so I bow to their ability to be more objective. I can only say in my behalf I was a cooperative Indian for more years than I was the chief. I thought the control I sought was control of me. Moves up the ladder paid the bills.

Because you have been a good teacher it does not necessarily follow that you will be a good head of a

142

school. As everywhere else in life, one is dogged by Parkinson's Law that we rise to our level of incompetence. Along with an intelligent concern and affection for the young, and a long list of other things, one must also take a kind of humility into that nifty, neatly slip-covered office, an ability to say "mea culpa." I think that I did, though "humility" would hardly be listed as my strong point by either friend or foe.

My first administrative job was at Springside School in Philadelphia, as director of the Middle School. The boys and I lived there for five years and whatever W. C. Fields said about Philadelphia I second the motion. In five years I was quite literally never once introduced anywhere to anyone, by anyone as "Jean Harris." It was always "This is Mrs. Harris. Mrs. Harris is the director of the Middle School at Springside."

I never got a run down on how everyone else in the room made a living, but "director of the Middle School at Springside" was part of my name for those five years. My sons loved, and still love, Philadelphia, a very important plus, and Springside was a splendid school and a fine place to begin my administrative experience, so what's to complain? I remember it as the place and time when I began to be a nonperson.

My years at Springside, 1966 to 1971, as director of the Middle School were those very disruptive years nationally when young people were breading out of the cocoons of the fifties and early sixties, protesting against the Vietnam War, protesting about what we were doing to the environment, and, most frightening of all for parents, beginning to use drugs. It was a whole new experience for suburban parents and teachers and it marks the time, on my calendar certainly, when parents began turning more and more to the schools and saying "do something."

From those years on, teachers and administrators in what are still our "better" schools began to play roles they had not bargained for and still aren't really prepared for. There were many times as I sat in my office and parents poured out their fears and frustrations about their children and ended with "What shall we do?" that I was tempted to cry "How in the hell should I know!" I often said, "If I had all the answers I suppose I'd have two perfect children. In the long run the answer depends upon love, common sense, and the energy it takes to say 'no.' "

I don't think we've grown one bit wiser in the last fifteen years about how to raise children. Instead, we've kept backing down and learning to accept what they want—before we've taught them what all the options are. Worst of all, we've taught them that "love" means lying for them and making excuses for them. It's something many parents do today. My notes from parent conferences read like the parent-conference notes of every school administrator along the East Coast during those years:

"One mother came in to tell me she 'knows for a fact that some of our eighth grade girls are smoking pot.' She said her daughter had seen them 'on several occasions.' She refused to give any names because 'One of the families involved have been friends for years. I know them well enough to know they wouldn't do much about it anyway, and I don't want to spoil the friendship. I think you ought to do something about it, Mrs. Harris.' I assured her I couldn't react to anything that vague and therefore on behalf of the school I couldn't help." In one three-month period there were eleven different parents who came for conferences that ended with "But I can't say anymore because of what the other girls will do to

Ethel—or Mary," or whatever the daughter's name was "and anyway I just don't want to get involved."

Another mother rushed into my office one day, very upset, having just come from a town meeting where drugs were being discussed. She had asked the speaker what a responsible citizen should do if he knew a person was selling pot. The speaker had said, "Report that person at once to the police."

The mother had been told by her daughter of a boy in the neighborhood who sold pot. Mother gave me the boy's name and urged me to call the police. "If I called them myself it would destroy my daughter's confidence in me. I promised her I wouldn't tell." The school became a dumping ground for everyone's nasty little secrets, or worse, nasty little rumors, and then Mother went home feeling cleansed.

We scurried around to find good films and convincing speakers about drugs but there weren't many to be found. Most of them simply served to widen the credibility gap, and one of our speakers, a doctor and parent of one of the students, gave them the "I'd rather see them use pot than alcohol" line, which didn't help very much.

In a memo to Miss Potter, headmistress of Springside, dated April 1969, I wrote, "This is my last parent conference on the subject of pot. If anyone else brings it up I will refer them to you. I don't know in my own mind what the answers to the pot questions are, and I have played the go-between, detective, and villain for the eighth grade to a very tiresome degree this year. Next year I'm going to try to be an educator again." I noted at the end of the memo that while I was writing it three disgruntled eighth graders had come into my office and prefaced their conversation with, "Why does the school always have to get involved in everything we do?"

Why indeed! I've asked myself the same question many times. The answer I think is that adults and children are both frightened: There aren't many social rules anymore to make them feel safe. They all want someone to blame for their discomfort, and someone to make them feel more secure. They often ask the school and the school administrator to play both roles. It wasn't without reason that I often talked to the girls about our "schizophrenic world."

Eleven years later I had apparently changed my definition of what an "educator" is, or is supposed to do. The last letter I dictated on Monday, March 10, 1980, was to an old and dear friend of Madeira's who had written me a lovely, rambling, philosophical letter about integrity and had asked me for more copies of my speech on the subject. I told him briefly of the sadness of having to expel four seniors just two months before graduation and added:

> I like to believe that morality on this campus has now bottomed out, and there is no place to go but up. It is the top item on my agenda for the rest of the time I am here. A Merit Scholar without a conscience is no scholar at all.

In a tragedy where irony has run rampant this is perhaps the greatest irony of all. Within hours after she wrote that, the earnest lady who wrote it was indicted for second degree murder! I keep thinking, with a sad smile, of the old Russian peasant saying "When the fox preaches the passion, farmer watch out for your sheep." I wonder how many people since that March night, standing with a drink in the hand, have said, "Who the hell was she . . ."

I keep on preaching, knowing that I am not the fox, but forgetting sometimes that many people now think that I am.

Twice in my naiveté have I told parents, without couching it in "maybes" or "possiblys," that I thought their daughter was using drugs. In each case I believed there was no doubt, but in each case I couldn't have proved it in court.

The first mother already knew about it and wasn't worried. "Everybody talks about it because the drab, square little people around here have always been jealous of me, and their daughters are jealous of Jackie. They're ratting on her because they're jealous and I think it's absolutely shitty of them!"

She added, "Of course I can't make Jackie do anything she doesn't want to do. The only approach is to make the children know it isn't chic to smoke pot anymore—people aren't doing it." These were her exact words. Unfortunately, the only reason it isn't "chic" today is because it's so commonplace.

The second time, at another school, one of the seniors slipped out of her chair onto the floor and lay there, sound asleep, in the middle of an assembly, practically under the nose of the speaker. At the end of the assembly her friends nudged her and woke her and she did her best to leave the auditorium before I could say "Please go to my office." She stayed there until her mother arrived. Mother listened to what the girl had done and said, "She was bored."

In the course of relating what had happened I had used the term "spaced out." Mother's second sentence was "I'll see you in court. And you better be able to prove that in court." The case never materialized because I think it must finally have become evident to the family how very deeply involved in drugs the girl was.

One of the country's most prestigious boarding schools was sued by the parents of a student expelled for using pot. The parents' case was "if the school had been doing its job properly, and instilling the right values, the student wouldn't have used pot." In the last fifteen years private schools have spent thousands and thousands of dollars on litigation of drug related offenses. The young haven't been served, the use of marijuana hasn't abated, tuitions have gone up, and untold hours of teaching and administrative time have been wasted.

Since 1968 I have read virtually every article and book on the subject of marijuana that I could find, and have read or given many of them to students. Hy, who had very strong convictions about the danger of pot, sent me anything of value on the subject that came to his attention. In fact, he always sent extra copies so that I would send one to each of my sons. I have talked with doctors, policemen, and psychiatrists on the subject, and had them talk to students. I have expelled students for selling, using, or possessing pot on campus because it was against not only federal or state laws, but against the clearly stated and written rules of all the schools I have worked in.

What I have done many educators and parents all over the country have done. Today the TV program "60 Minutes" tells me that marijuana is the largest cash crop in the states of Hawaii and California. A number of (more than five) Madeira students have told me, quite openly and ingenuously, that parents of their friends in some of America's poshest neighborhoods "sell pot." "But they're really very nice people, Mrs. Harris. They'd never sell bad stuff." What will happen is what has always happened. When enough people do "the wrong thing" it becomes "the right thing." The words "progress" and "evolution" both carry with them the mythology of "getting better."

We look at the apes in the zoo or picture a Neanderthal man dragging his mate by the hair, and we look at ourselves in the mirror and think, "Fantastic! It all came out so well!" Since change is the one thing you can bank on perhaps it's a good myth to cling to; far wiser though to accept Lewis Thomas's article of faith "that we humans are a profoundly immature species, only now beginning the process of learning how to learn. . . . Young and old, we are always students in an introductory class."

At the three schools where I have served as an administrator there was a building that could have been used for a small day-care center. Each was a good building, homey, attractive, a place where I would have let my own children attend nursery school. In each case I was willing to do the work required to start a nursery, to find the money, and to make it part of the curriculum for students to staff it. In each case there were working mothers nearby who needed such a facility. In each case the building did not meet federal OSHA standards about how many square feet and how many toilets go to make a good day-care center, so the potential came to nothing. The more we talk about individuality the more standardized we become. To too many people individuality means "anything you get, I get," whether it's floor space or toilets or a college diploma.

Private schools are especially big on "individuality," "individual attention," "the importance of the individual," and "helping the individual to achieve her full potential." The very difficult part, the part that most students and parents and board members everywhere can't accept, is that consistency is the first casualty when you're a firm believer in individuality.

"Mrs. Harris is too emotional and she isn't consistent," were the two complaints brought to me by the president and vice-president of the board at Madeira when they gave me my new contract and a large raise. I told them the first criticism was certainly deserved and I would work on it, and I did, very hard. To the second criticism I could only promise they would hear more of the same as I continued to make as honest an evaluation of each student and each situation as I could.

The same thing never happened twice. It was only on the surface that things looked the same. Decisions that sounded "inconsistent" were not made precipitously, and some may have been wrong, but the school's philosophy was to have high moral standards for all students and to value and honor and encourage individuality, and that's what was done. It is not an easy combination of goals to achieve, again because the lines are not clearly drawn between what we want and what we think we want.

Of the four schools where I have worked, one gave grades and had an academic honor roll, one gave grades but never had an academic honor roll, one gave grades and was about to give up its honor roll last I heard, and one gave no grades at all, only written comments. The stated philosophical goals of all four schools were almost identical. "Equality" and "individuality" were the educational passwords in the middle sixties, and all through the seventies, private as well as public schools rode off in every direction pursuing them.

Madeira, for philosophical reasons I have never heard explained, gives elaborate silver bowls and endless ribbons for riding but awards no prizes or recognition of any kind for academic achievement. It won't even allow Yale or Harvard to award a book to an outstanding student. If one is simply motivated to do one's best academically, why not the same motivation on a horse? There is a splendid, illogical smugness about the old riders of Madeira that refuses to be confused by logic. I was reminded many times that "the riders give more money." I'm afraid it will always be so. It was a "riding" member of the board who said to me with venom in her voice, "It is obscene to suggest selling one inch of these four hundred acres for endowment." She never suggested that it was obscene to ask a good teacher and father of three to live on $10,000 a year.

By the time I reached the Thomas School I could defend, even though it still wasn't my first choice, the school's recently adopted system of no grades at all, only comments. Grades had become so inflated that "average" had squeezed out the Cs and become a B on almost every campus in the country. The old bell-shaped curve, for good or for ill, had disappeared with the whooping crane.

Rowayton,
Connecticut:
Farewell to Thomas

I moved to Connecticut in the fall of 1971 to take over as head of the Thomas School. The school had just been refused accreditation by the New England Association of Schools and Colleges for a long list of reasons.

Among others, the budget indicated that there would be a $78,000 deficit that year and no one had any idea how it would be covered. The alumnae were all mad at someone or something; the cocktail party circuit said the school wouldn't open another year. Many of the school's old records and reports had no dates on them and grades were often noted on the back of an old envelope in Miss Thomas's careful script, so preparing a transcript was sometimes an all-day affair. Renaissance history was being taught in the seventh, eighth, and tenth grades because some of the alumnae remembered what fun it had been to dress up in thirteenth century costumes and have splendid pageants on the shores of Long Island Sound, and the American history classes were still reading Muzzey, virtually unchanged since I had used it thirty years before! Fortunately it went out of print the second year I was there.

All those things notwithstanding, there was a sense

of community about the place, some fine girls, a few master teachers, and a beautiful plant to work with. (Besides being beautiful the plant had a very large demand mortgage whose interest rate jumped from 5½ to 8 percent one day in 1973!) The board consisted of some very decent people who were willing to give the place one more good try at survival against rough odds. They were completely honest with me about the school's problems—to the extent that they knew them. No one can ever predict what various members of the alumnae will do at any school, but especially a school that had been founded fifty years before "for the exceptional child," meaning, from what I saw, exceptionally bright, exceptionally dull, exceptionally talented, and exceptionally trying— some of each. I too was willing to take the gamble because the experience would be valuable, it would be wonderfully gratifying if we succeeded, and Philadelphia was a dead end. I could stay and become the grand old lady of the Middle School if I lived long enough, but that didn't sound like an appealing option.

Many splendid things happened at Thomas. The school was small enough so that we could do things together, mixing ages from twelve to eighteen, moving school to the Delaware Water Gap for a beautiful week in October with a wonderfully enthusiastic faculty happy to cooperate, enjoying almost a family closeness. Unfortunately, it was too small to pay its bills and ultimately the board with my strong recommendation voted to close the school and give its assets to another girls' school, the Low-Heywood School in Stamford. The school's last year and its closing were remarkably orderly and productive, especially in view of the difficulties thrown in its path by a small but very vocal and emotional group of alumnae.

153

I had no sooner arrived at Thomas than letters arrived threatening no support until a teacher who had been fired the year before was reinstated. That another teacher was now under contract to teach the man's classes, that the man had been introduced to me once and been unconscionably rude was of no matter. One woman assured me the school would never get "another dime" until it rehired four of her favorite teachers who, over a period of seven years, had bit the dust. One had left because of poor health, one now lived in Florida, another was working happily in New York—details—get them back. Fortunately, "another dime" was about all she had ever given so the next one wasn't missed. One alumna whose daughter was a senior when I arrived hadn't paid her tuition bills for two years. Other alumnae thought it was "absolutely rotten" of me to make an issue of money with a nice old graduate of Thomas. "Give her a scholarship." There are many alumnae—not just at Thomas—who can't see why it "costs anything" to have a couple more students around, as long as "the teachers and things are there anyway." How the teachers will get paid simply doesn't concern them. The alumna in question finally gave us a lien on her house for the $6,900 she owed us when her daughter graduated. When her house was sold we were sixth on the list of lien holders and got nothing. Later, when a very emotional group of alumnae and neighbors were holding public meetings to "save Thomas," the lady in question very publicly signed a pledge of $1,500 for the school if we stayed open another year. If you are going to help save a private institution you profess to love, something in addition to your heart has to be in the right place!

In the early spring of 1972 I asked the seniors what preferences they had for a commencement speaker and what subjects they might like to hear about. The replies tell much about what was happening in schools that year. There were mixed returns on preferences, though "poetry reading" was first. One girl summed up for all of them the subjects they didn't want. "I don't want to hear about drugs, war, pollution, apathy in students, the generation gap, women's lib, college, or sex!" I was a little tired of that list too, but while you could pick the graduation speaker you couldn't pick each day's traumas and crises. Enrollment in private schools was falling in 1972-1973 and admissions policies in a school like Thomas were very elastic. We ran the gamut from happy, well-adjusted, varsity hockey type Merit Scholars to some pretty troubled young ladies who brought a lot of their trouble with them. There were some all-American types with sad problems too, like the one who left to have a baby, gave it up for adoption, and then didn't go to her senior prom because "I don't know anyone to ask."

The everyday problems of running a school were no different those four years at Thomas than at most schools. There was constant agitation for a smoking room. Just at the moment when there was proof positive that smoking was harmful, school after school knuckled under and gave the kids their way. The principal of a large public high school in Connecticut said, "We know it's crazy, but at least this way they don't lock themselves in the lavatories and rip the fixtures off the wall." My firm "No" remained a firm "No" at Thomas and the students came back with their favorite argument, "You're a hypocrite if you don't let us smoke because you know we're going to do it anyway."

Clothing was a big item which you tried to downplay because there were always eager candidates for martyrdom if you made it too much of an issue, ready to fight for their God-given right to be dirty, sloppy and inappropriate. At Springside the girls wore uniforms but the imaginative young could think of hundreds of ways to sidestep the intent of the dress code and still be "legally" within bounds.

At Thomas I tried by example and gentle persuasion to upgrade appearances and finally had to resort to a written plea to the parents because the message was coming back "Mrs. X brought her daughter to look at the school but wouldn't consider sending little Sally where students looks so ghastly." Harvard can get away with it, but a struggling little day school had to dress up for company. We were on the road to respectable compromise by the time it closed.

Thomas's last graduation was a beautiful one, out in the garden with the rhododendron in full bloom. The students were all accepted at other schools for the next year; most of the teachers, not all, had new jobs. Two retiring teachers who would have been virtually destitute were given generous retirement settlements from the sale of the school property. All teachers were given severance pay based on years of service to the school; Miss Darling, in her late eighties, who had lived at the school since she had retired years before as the music teacher, went to a retirement home run by her church, with her rent paid by the school; and $250,000 was given to Low-Heywood-Thomas. Mildred Dunnock, an old friend of the school, read from T.S. Eliot's "East Coker."

There were tears, but it ended in an orderly, dignified way, not in chaos and tragedy as it might have.

Virginia:
Headmistress

1.

It is hard to be the head of a boarding school, and it's particularly hard if you don't have a wife. You have to be twice as energetic—and hug the dog when you feel hurt. Better still you should be very tough and not feel hurt. Ask any good headmistress, and there are some fine ones, what she was like as a child and she'll tell you, "I was a tomboy, climbed trees, and played center field for the neighborhood team." Today she can down two double martinis at lunch and still go back to the meeting and remember what anyone said. While they were climbing trees I was playing house, and while they're ordering the second martini I'm still on my first whiskey sour. Maybe I should have admitted to myself after that first meeting of the Headmistresses Association of the East that I was no match for them. But I loved the challenge and I tackled the job with a will.

A headmistress is thought to be a "role model," and so she can be sometimes. I think I was willing to be one, but I wanted the role to be that of a woman first—a woman who happened to be a headmistress. I'm afraid that wasn't the model the Madeira board had agreed upon. At best the board was ambivalent.

I had said to the search committee before I came to Madeira, "Please know that I will work hard for the girls and for the school. But I will not marry Madeira. I will have a private life away from the school, a life that will refuel me. I will not live my life vicariously through the girls and their kind letters. I want to live life as fully as I hope each of them will." I'm sure no one was listening.

I have probably been told a hundred times, "You sure don't look like a headmistress." A child said it to me once and added most ingenuously, "You just look like somebody's mother." I would be willing to bet that no one ever told Ted Sizer of Andover, or Charlie Lord of St. Timothy's, or Emmet Wright of Woodberry Forest, "You sure don't look like a headmaster."

Headmasters come in all sizes, shapes, and ages—though the truth is they are often very attractive, gray, if at all, in just the right places, with leather elbow patches on the tweed jacket, a pretty wife from one of the Seven Sisters, and two adorable, apple-checked children—once in pinafores, now in hip-hugger jeans. If old dad lasts long enough at the job the apple-cheeked children can become very troubled, or very troublesome from being reminded so many times they are the headmaster's children, and a healthy number of the nifty wives are finally saying, "I'll be glad to run the bazaar, and have eighty for coffee, twenty-five for dinner, teach Latin, and proctor the library—as soon as I'm on the payroll. No tickee, no washee!" But whatever his other problems, and they are considerable by the very nature of his job, he is not expected to be physically unattractive.

Headmistresses still are. Bifocals, short cropped gray hair, big feet, short and waistless, or uncommonly tall and gangly, someone who kept rising on the educational ladder because she didn't get a better offer. It's terribly outdated and it was always inappropriate but it's still pervasive. Even grandparents who now tell you casually about the "nice boy" their granddaughter is living with still expect a Mrs. Chipsy type, safely married or safely unwanted, sitting in the headmistress's chair. And heaven knows, whatever the life-style of the students, their parents, and the board members may be it mustn't be hers. Hers is but to do or die.

I haven't any statistics, but as I think of the headmistresses I know today most are happily married, to what must be a very special fellow who puts up with the intrusions on their privacy and gives her the support that keeps her going. I don't know any bachelor headmasters.

I was not a stranger to the traumas and pressures of running a school or to family pressures when I arrived at Madeira, but by March 1980 I was growing less and less resilient. I fell harder and bounced back slower. There was never anyone there to catch the fall. I had been told by the board of directors of Madeira that I was their unanimous choice as head of the school. They had rung my bell, not I theirs, and they had pondered about their choice for over six months after their first interview with me, and they had checked into every corner of my life. They arranged a large reception for me where I was introduced to the school's constituency.

What I did not know until two years later was that they were still having a cat fight over the selection five minutes before the first guests arrived. I don't know if Hy played any part in their deliberations, or not. He certainly did two years later after his ill-timed but well meant acknowledgement of me in his book.

Shortly after it came out I was told by a board member, "You have no right *ever* during the school year to leave this campus on a weekend unless it is on school business."

It was spring 1979, the junior and senior students had unlimited weekends but the woman who worked seven days and nights a week to run that school was actually told by a popular member of the board that from September 5 to June 8 the parameters of her life were to be the Madeira campus. This from a woman who had professed friendship and support until the day she made this senseless pronouncement, right after her announcement in a board meeting that, "As far as I'm concerned you're on probation." Not one board member raised a voice in my behalf.

Not one board member protested. Not one board member asked the reason for her statement. Not one board member called later and said "Forget it—she's an idiot." The woman herself never responded to two letters from me, nor returned three phone calls. And another member of the board said, "Oh heavens, of course you aren't on probation." She refused three requests of mine to put that statement in writing. A student treated in the same arbitrary way would have brought suit. I was given a $5,000 raise and another year's contract but no civility and no apology.

In February 1980 I was given my fourth one-year contract and another $5,000 raise. I had gone to be headmistress of the Thomas School in Connecticut in the fall of 1971 knowing that it was a calculated risk as to whether the school could be salvaged. The board was well informed about the condition of the school—late in becoming so, but certainly honest with me. I went to Madeira believing I would have the active cooperation and support of the board and believing it was in a much stronger position than it was. In that respect the board hadn't been dishonest. They had simply been totally uninformed about what condition the school was in. And I was the messenger who brought the bad news.

Among other things, heads of private schools are mendicants, always shaking the tambourine, always in need of money, the reason being, by and large, that they charge what the traffic will bear, not what services rendered actually cost. If competitive schools can pay their bills charging $9,500 per year for tuition, room and board because they have invested endowment to cover at least part of their deficit, then Madeira had to keep its tuition within that ball park figure and spend the rest of the year in an annual fund drive. Half a million dollar deficits per year are not unusual in many secondary schools today—and that just pays the bills and adds nothing to endowment.

One member said, at my first board meeting in October 1977, in a half annoyed, half defensive tone, "Whadda ya mean Madeira needs money? I thought we had plenty of money." This was in response to my observation that Madeira was ten years behind comparable schools in building an endowment. Madeira's endowment in 1966 was $1,600,000. Eleven years later, after the halcyon days of fund raising had passed, it was $2,300,000. Nothing had been done to protect the school against tomorrow, and tomorrow was now bearing down upon it with a vengeance. The reaction of the then chairman of the board when I said we must start immediately to organize long-range planning was "If you start any long-range planning around here you'll tear the place apart." He was wrong. It only tore me apart.

When I expressed my strong conviction that we needed faculty housing an earnest old friend of the

161

school said, "What about those houses we built eight years ago?" There were three houses built then, making a total of eight houses and one decent apartment on a campus with 215 boarding students and another hundred day students. Two of those eight houses were lived in by maintenance people, one by the business manager who had no contact with the students, one by the headmistress, one by the assistant headmistress, one by the daughter of the school nurse, and two by full-time teachers. One of the two teachers was in the process of divorcing his wife in order to marry one of the Madeira seniors. There was no guidance counselor, no chaplain, and no adult living in four of the six dormitories.

In short, not one normal family situation was available to the girls on the entire four-hundred acre campus. From 4:30 P.M. until 8:00 A.M. the girls were virtuallly on their own. This does not mean there was chaos in the dorms. Miss Keyser, the retiring headmistress, was a strong taskmaster and a very hard worker and there was a very good system of student housemothers—but there was not a touch of the warmth of family life or close contact between generations, and little opportunity for faculty to come across as humans as well as pedagogues.

Ted Sizer, before he retired as headmaster of Andover, wrote in a thirty-three page report to the board of Andover (I doubt there were many members of the board at Madeira who would *read* a thirty-three page report!):

House counseling is the most sophisticated, demanding academic job on this campus. Unless a student is "together" in the dormitory his or her French, or algebra, or history, or field hockey will suffer. . . . House counseling isn't merely supervision: it's education . . . it is a central part of the fabric of this institution . . . Accessibility, caring, sensitivity, genuine interest, the courage to be condemnatory, to be the taskmaster or mistress as well as the readiness to be a friend: these qualities can't be categorized by "hours on duty" or items on a list to be checked off. But they are the heart of a good residential education.

Mr. Sizer is 100 percent correct. His statement is simple common sense to anyone who has taken the time to spend a single day and night on a boarding school campus, especially a day in the past ten years. I had said essentially the same thing to Madeira's board for almost three years. The reality of the message is expensive, however, and Madeira's board simply chose over the years to ignore it. I am told they have recently completed housing I urged eight years ago.

I immediately set up a system of faculty advisors for each student and an Adult-on-Duty who used my office from 3:30 Friday until 10:00 P.M. Sunday so that every girl leaving or returning to campus checked into a warm, living-room like atmosphere (the Madeira dorms have no living rooms), often with a fire in the fireplace and always proctored by a member of the faculty or Mrs. Harris. It was one of many new burdens I placed upon the faculty, since it meant a long drive back to campus for most of them—and sitter problems for their children.

In time they began to bring their children, which was an important plus for the campus, and the girls began to enjoy seeing the math teacher doing her needlepoint, or reading to her children, or watching a football game, and that office became a popular

163

gathering place on weekends. They even came down in their pajamas and did their homework in front of the fire.

I told the school nurse that I wanted always to be told of any injuries the girls sustained; and, if they needed to be taken to the hospital any time at night, I wanted to take them. I watched a number of bones be set, a thumb sewed back, and heard a girl be told in the gentlest and saddest conversation I have ever heard in my life that she was indeed an alcoholic. In a very weary, little-girl voice she responded, "I wasn't sure but I was beginning to be afraid so . . ." And I heard a doctor, whose license to practice should at least have been temporarily withdrawn, say in the most callous possible way to a terrified youngster who had been burned on the face, "Get her to a plastic surgeon—it's too late for me to help"—and he turned on his heels and walked away.

Picture yourself on a campus seven days and seven nights a week with a small group of adults—maybe five on a good night and two or three other nights—and 215 teenagers you care very much about, every one of whom has some kind of a problem, from a mother dying of cancer, to a playboy father, to a dad out of work or a beau who never called, or a D— on a paper she worked her heart out for, and tell me where you begin. I know where you end.

My first year at Madeira I gave diplomas to girls I barely knew. From then on I taught a weekly class to freshmen and I made every effort to spend time with the seniors—first in half-hour conferences in my office, then when time interfered I began to invite groups of day students to lunch in four or fives—and ask the boarders to come by in groups of three, four, or five about 9:00 P.M. for cocoa and cookies. The conversation began rather awkwardly. They were mixed groups of girls, some "in" members and some "out" members, but in a very short time they found a subject they cared about and the conversation often went until 11:00 or 11:30, with me walking the girls back to their dorms. It was obvious that they hungered for conversations with adults, and while most of the people on campus, especially a splendid dean of students and the young head of publications, did yeoman duty all hours of the day and night, there simply weren't enough adults to go around.

I urged the board to borrow $250,000 at once (at 8½ percent) and make room for trained adults and families to live near the girls. I had, and still have, great respect for the student housemother system, and for the right of boarding school faculty to a modicum of privacy and normal living. Many boarding schools have too much "togetherness." We had simply gone the other extreme. I even had plans drawn up that would have put space in three existing buildings to far better use and in the process would have added four excellent, well-placed faculty apartments. Unfortunately, by the time I arrived, the school's much touted solar-heated science building was about to fall apart and the next three years of the board's attention were spent trying unsuccessfully to put Humpty Dumpty together again.

I did not lack courage when I went to Madeira. I was quite willing to put my neck on the block and make whatever decisions needed to be made. And I knew what many of those decisions were—but no one can run a school (or a business either unless you own it) without a board with the courage and integrity to back the person to whom they hand the responsibility.

When I arrived at Madeira it had never, to the best of my ability to find out, been evaluated by an outside group of its peers and equals. There was a provincialism, a smugness about it that made it feel wonderfully safe about its superiority and very closeminded about "the real world."

State accreditation requires 180 days of school. Madeira juniors, because of a unique program, a six-week Christmas holiday and a two-week period on Capitol Hill, had less than 130 days of classes my first year at Madeira. The library was seriously inadequate and often used as a big recreation room. A once fine riding program was beginning to deteriorate but the male members of the board were too intimidated by a few wealthy riders to do anything about it; and as a final note there had never been a funded maintenance program set up so the beautiful fifty-year-old buildings had very leaky basements, tile roofs that could go at any time, and furniture and equipment that was falling apart and uninventoried.

At the end of my first three months at Madeira I felt a kind of urgency to get moving that bordered on the frantic. By the end of the first year I had cut Christmas vacation in half, brought Latin back into the curriculum, brought mid-year and final exams back into being, increased already taxed faculty responsibility by setting up an advisor-advisee system for every student, changed the administration of the school to include a dean of students and an academic dean, written a faculty handbook, rewritten the student handbook, begun to organize board committees for long-range planning, and begun to pull school files and records together.

My first year with the seniors was a nightmare. They had come to terms with Miss Keyser's style and wanted no part of mine. A favorite "Madeira tradition" as they called it was an arrangement whereby each class chose a "class hymn" and the assistant

166

headmistress led them in contests to see which class could shriek its hymn the loudest. This was called chapel.

When one of the student singing groups sang some original lyrics at a Mother's Day luncheon—lyrics that were tasteless and offensive in the extreme—and the singing itself had been unrehearsed and sloppy at best, I met with the girls and told them I hoped they would continue to sing but with two caveats: (1) that they practice before giving a performance, and (2) that they not use words that were inappropriate for them and an embarrassment to their audience.

Various versions of our conversation quickly spread across the country and all hell broke loose. One very feisty and thoroughly uninformed young lady wrote, "Maybe your priorities for the school and the students are misplaced. In my opinion the headmistress should deal with major issues and leave the harmless issues to the discretion of the students. You should not restrict all aspects of the students' lives. Songs represent a release and a form of entertainment for the students."

I was constantly being told that shrieking and screaming in chapel and in the dining room were "our only release—you can't take it away from us . . . it's a Madeira tradition." The four hundred glorious acres they could walk, ride, and scream their heads off in were rarely traveled by any except the horseback riders.

It took three years and a lot of strength and determination, but I brought music back to Madeira while I was there—the joy of it and the beauty of it— something totally missing when I arrived. It isn't the sort of thing I had expected to have to fight for.

It also took three years of unpleasantness and overt rudeness from students and parents alike, even several

167

board members, to turn what had been called "Mothers' Day" and "Fathers' Day" (there was no parents' association at Madeira) into school weekends where faculty, students, and parents were *on* campus getting to know one another and sharing their school experiences.

When I arrived in 1977 the day consisted of a quick run-through of morning classes, a box lunch, a quick cocktail party with the faculty, and then two days of partying and shopping with old Dad or Mom in Georgetown. My recommendation that everyone stay on campus for a father-daughter dinner was met with howls of protest and open hostility. I was destroying "another Madeira tradition." I was simply introducing a little common sense.

But in April 1980, after I was gone and Hy was gone, Fathers' Day had become Fathers' Weekend and it went off as I had spent three years struggling to have it. One kind father wrote and thanked me.

2.

There was not one single move I made at Madeira that did not have an unpleasant backlash. When I wrote the students late in August and asked them all to bring a few dozen daffodil bulbs back with them, to start what I hope may now be a tradition to fill the campus with spring flowers, I received one letter. It didn't say "What a nice idea." It said:

September 8

Dear Jean,
    The epistle of the daffodils was not well received in this household and I have heard of similiar reaction in a couple of other households.

168

Though the gals sometimes act like second graders, I suspect they react better to pleas couched in adult terms. Withal, I cannot quibble with a Lady Bird Johnson effort and will send Audrey some bulbs when they come on the market in these environs.

I sent a good-natured reply to the effect that I wasn't "talking down" to anyone, it was just my way of expressing myself, and signed it "Rebecca of Sunnybrook Farm." She wrote back,, "Dear Rebecca, You're a neat gal—loved your letter, thanks, . . ." But everything, every move, had to be explained, however simple and innocent it seemed to me when I made it.

Even Christmas became something to fight about. For four years the girls had left school the day before Thanksgiving and returned in January, having had a six-week "Christmas break." In 1978 I changed the calendar back to a three-week Christmas break, and then I set about trying to resurrect the Christmas traditions, as Madeira had once celebrated them. I was reminded almost immediately that not everyone at Madeira was a Christian and wasn't I being anti-Semitic. I have probably told more little WASPs about the beautiful festival of Hanukah than any other Episcopalian could, without her own televised talk show, so my conscience was very clear on that score.

I was open to all suggestions and the deans and I spent many hours figuring out a calendar of events, trying not to step on any academic toes, trying to keep the Glee Club happy (that was *very* important to me), find time to gather greens and teach the girls to make wreaths, decide when to light the big tree (and should it be *required* for the day girls) and how to serve a turkey dinner to four hundred people in the gym without lines that were unmanageable, etc.

No two people remembered the "traditions" in quite the same way except for the traditional Christmas story that *everyone* remembered Miss Madeira reading to the girls each year. And they remembered it with great affection. I was given Miss Madeira's own copy of it by a dear and generous lady who handed it to me as though she were turning over the Holy Grail.

It was called "How Come Christmas," charming in its day perhaps—if you were white—but written in an "all dem chilluns is gwine wait fo dat old Sandy Claws." At one time I would have read it with the same good will and innocence that Miss Madeira read it and her girls enjoyed it. It made me realize in the starkest possible way how smug what we called "innocence" could be and was. Today it would be unthinkable to read, an affront not only to the black girls but to all of us. Needless to say, by omitting it from our celebration I lost brownie points I sorely needed. At the last minute I searched for a Christmas story that might be new to the girls and read them Damon Runyon's "Dancing Dan's Christmas." They didn't like it, so the next year I read them "Gift of the Magi" and they were quite content.

How do you figure out a generation of young women who play "Why Don't We Do It in the Road" on their stereos and still sit enchanted by "Gift of the Magi"? I think for some of them it was the first hearing. One of the girls asked who Noah was, so anything is possible.

By the second year everyone seemed more relaxed about my intentions toward Madeira's traditions, a madrigal group had been formed, the girls who really loved music had been enticed back into the Glee

Club, the "Wums" and Humditties" and "Agonies" were better than ever, and the wonderful, spontaneous humor and warmth of the girls were reflected in their delightful decorations in each dormitory.

It was Christmas again at Madeira, even if the headmistress was still suspect in the eyes of many. I baked cookies for the entire school when we lit the tree in Main, and the bigger one at the Chapel was decorated with toys for youngsters at Children's Hospital. Some of the girls gave a party for children from the Alley Library.

Giving, as I knew but relearned at Madeira, is not a God-given instinct. It is learned. And we have to be reminded of it from time to time—in fact, educated in the ways of it—in order to be thoughtful about it. My first fall at Madeira the girls (all of them) contributed a total of $27 to the United Fund. If they didn't know any better than this, we had short-changed them. There are legitimate reasons for not giving to the United Fund or to anything else if you aren't so inclined, but this was a thoughtless, uninformed kind of not giving, unacceptable behavior in my opinion in young women being educated to be productive and aware of their world.

There were weeks when they cashed as much as $5,000 to $6,000 in personal checks at the school bank. They thought nothing of calling a cab to deliver $150 worth of ice cream from Baskin-Robbins.

Working through the student council and especially the senior class, we talked a good deal about values and needs and self-indulgence. I added a strong suggestion in the student handbook that $40 to $50 per month was a very generous allowance at boarding school. Some parents appreciated the suggestion, a predictable group said, "Who the hell are you . . ."

171

We investigated community needs, saw where United Fund monies were used, and in two years the girls' contributions had hit five figures. I believe that is so, though I haven't the statistics with me. I think the figure that first year was a clear reflection of how much the girls needed adults in their lives.

My last school year at Madeira started sadly because of a careless accident, one I could have avoided had I had the strength and courage to banish another "old Madeira tradition" from the campus when I wanted to. In spite of all the extenuating circumstances I never considered myself less than fully responsible, because, as Mr. Truman was fond of saying, "The buck stops here."

A number of years ago a group called the BHs was founded at Madeira. BH stood for "Brazen Hussies." I happen to know the decent woman who founded it. I met her later, and I know the group was started for fun and high-jinks, to add a little life and humor to the boredom of campus life at a time when students had only two weekends off campus per semester, and time must have hung heavy for active teenagers. Members' names were supposed to be secret, but by the time I arrived they seemed to be widely known, at least by the seniors. To be a BH was considered the "in" thing to be.

Depending upon the year, and the members, the pranks played by the BHs ranged from totally innocent, to annoying, to downright destructive. A few years before I arrived that they had "rearranged" the curtain pulleys in the school theater so that $1,500 was needed to put them right again. The BHs paid the bill. While I was there they collected all the toothbrushes on campus and strung them from trees, moved every piece of furniture out of my office and set it up in the quad with a sign that read, "Just

172

Airing Out the Administration," hung silly signs out to welcome parents to the campus, wrapped my house in foil and tied it with a big red ribbon, all foolish stuff that everyone seemed to enjoy. Quite harmless.

I entered into the spirit of fun wholeheartedly, and even won a prize for the best Halloween costume one year without anyone knowing who I was. Part of the costume was black net stockings, and though the rest of it was a weird combination of anything I could find to cover up in, they agreed, "She's got good legs whoever she is." I had written one of the faculty follies we put on while I was there. The faculty needed rehearsals and another night at school like a hole in the head, but they were good sports and we brightened up two Februaries with them.

On one of the follies nights it was snowing so hard the faculty all had to spend the night on campus filling the infirmary and any faculty house with a spare bed. We let the girls stay out of their dorms until 11:00 that night to enjoy it. I will always remember one of the girls lying in the snow in front of Main, making angel wings with her arms in the snow, watching the snow come down through the branches of one of the big elm trees, with light from the buildings making it all sparkle, and saying. "Oh, Mrs. Harris. Isn't it wonderful!"

Somewhere in its history the BHs activities had become involved in Red and White Day, a day in early fall when all the new girls were accepted into the Red or White Teams. Special freshmen were picked to be initiated. BHs were assigned a new girl, made her a costume based on some theme, and then late in the afternoon there was a cookout for all freshmen and seniors at the cabin. The BHs made a list of any freshman who walked across the oval, or went in the senior's special entrance to the dining room, or committed any other faux pas that would bring them to senior attention. Freshmen hoped to get on the list. It was an early foot in the door to be one of the "in" group.

Red and White Day that last year began with the BHs waking at the crack of dawn, waking the freshmen on their list, taking them over near the swimming pool, blindfolding them, smearing them with something sticky, like shampoo or vaseline, or even peanut butter, then hosing them down and sending them shrieking and squealing back to their dorms. They had in years past even been made to climb the fence into the pool area where they were thrown into the pool in the dark. Some had even been tied to trees.

Miss Keyser, the retiring headmistress, had told me something about the BHs, mentioned the damage done to the theater, but said, on the whole they were a harmless "vent" and an accepted part of Madeira. Jean Gisriel (Giz) whom I had made the dean of students told me about their activities in greater detail and together we made up a list of rules the girls must follow if the BHs were to continue.

It was an awkward thing for me to do, because, as a freshman, I would have found no pleasure in being part of it and would happily have been left out. I wonder if that isn't true of many of the girls, but we make being "included" so important. The first rule was that the BHs must inform the night guard when they were going to be out of their dorms after 10:00 P.M. Secondly they could never climb into the pool area. Third, if their pranks became destructive they would not only pay the damages but risk suspension, and under no condition were they ever to tie one another to trees.

Giz didn't tell them; but it was also arranged that

when the guard was informed, she would be told by him so two adults would be up and in the area while the BHs went into action. Giz got up at 2:00 or 3:00 in the morning enough times to say to me, "If the guard and I go on meeting this way, I'm going to have to buy some new nightgowns." It was, in my opinion, the ultimate indulgence of the young, without their knowing it. The only thing I could say in its favor is that it was safer than it had been before. Or so I thought.

The night before Red and White Day, Giz reviewed the rules with the girls and was assured no one would get hurt. The next morning at about 4:00 A.M. as the BHs gathered to wake the new girls, one of them remembered she hadn't brought any shampoo or vaseline with her so she ran back to her bathroom to get it. Her roommate was senior class president and they shared a connecting bathroom with two other seniors.

So as not to wake anyone she went in the dark and grabbed the shampoo, only it turned out not to be shampoo. It was Vanisol, a plastic bottle of a liquid used to sanitize the toilets. It was 14 percent hydrochloric acid. By the time she caught up with the others all the new girls had been blindfolded, thank God, and were so smeared with shampoo and vaseline that the Vanisol barely touched them.

When a few girls began to complain, "Hey, this smells funny, and it burns," the seniors took off the blindfolds, hosed the girls down, and sent them back to their dorms to take showers.

Two girls were cold and didn't want to be hosed so they ran ahead and jumped in the shower. One of them didn't realize at the time that she had been badly burned on the face. She came out of the shower rubbing her face and saying, "I can't get this sticky stuff off." She wasn't in any pain, but she was rubbing off her own skin. When the other girls saw her they rushed her to the infirmary, the nurse called me and I took her at once to the hospital.

And this is when the doctor had his one sentence for the child's mother, who met us there, "Get her to a plastic surgeon." He is near the top of my list of people who should not be permitted to practice their chosen trades.

Both mother and child were wonderfully brave and wonderfully calm, and last I knew, except for one small spot, her face has healed and is fine, but that terrible morning we didn't know that it would.

When mother had left daughter I did what I had done for fourteen years and ran to the phone to call Hy. His calmness and reassurance was catching and helped me to get through the two long weeks that followed with television cameras all over the campus, and irate parents saying, "What are you going to do to the girls who did it?" Hy told me exactly what would and did happen.

"Jean, she's young and the young body has wonderful recuperative powers. It will probably heal itself largely. She'll have tender skin, and have to stay out of the sun, maybe for the rest of her life, but you will probably see most of it heal itself."

There were, as I have explained, several people on campus who wanted the headmistress's job, and her head as well. I'm told it was one of them who alerted the press immediately. I can remember saying to one of the press people who kept calling and trying to get some kind of inside information that didn't exist, "The girls in this school give just over 100,000 hours a year of volunteer service to the city of Washington and environs. As far as I know this has never brought you running to Madeira for pictures. Now suddenly

176

there is a tragic accident, nothing more, and we're red hot news. Come and see the good things that happen on purpose, not the sad thing that happened by accident."

The child who grabbed the Vanisol was from El Salvador. Her family had been moved to Florida for safety but her father still lived between El Salvador and the United States. It was a shaky time for him personally, and what should be done about his daughter became more complicated than might otherwise have been. Lawyers quickly got into the act, as lawyers do. I met with the school lawyer, the family, and the family's lawyer and before we could make any suggestions the family said they were taking her out and putting her in another school.

I'm happy to say she had a successful senior year in her new school. I think the girl who was hurt recovered as well as she did certainly in large part because her family was so calm, and so supportive, and put its energy into making her better instead of heading right to the courts. It was a sobering experience for the entire school. Had I stayed another year I'm not sure what I would have done about the BHs, but initiations would have been out. They are good-hearted girls, and would not hurt someone deliberately.

The day the girl from El Salvador left was one of the longest days I spent at Madeira. All her things were packed and down in the front hall, stereo, tennis racquets, radio, books, clothes, a large collection of boxes, and suitcases. Mother and father had flown in to get her and rented a car at the airport to come and pick her up.

The only problem was that where the child lived in El Salvador, mother and father had always driven her to the airport in a tiny sports car convertible, while her suitcases followed in a servant-driven station wagon. Her parents had no idea how much was packed to go with her. They arrived at Madeira in another tiny sports car convertible and had to return to the airport and rent a station wagon. The girls sat in the front hall and wept with her until mother and father came back for the second time. Why on earth I didn't put her in my car and follow them I don't know. It didn't occur to me until just now.

To the students I was often much too strict and hardnosed. One of them eagerly told reporters how I banished oranges and crackers from their diet for several weeks because after many reminders and warnings they still threw orange peels and cracker wrappers around the campus. I tried to explain that wasn't "discipline": it was "training," like making the puppy use newspaper instead of the carpet— training, I would like to add in a very loud voice, "that should have been taken care of at home."

To some parents who believed any casual remark their daughter made, especially if it were critical or derogatory, I was much too casual about discipline. An alumna wrote a few weeks before I left Madeira, "I have it on good authority that Mrs. Harris is lax and disinterested in discipline."

I had spent thirty-five years of my life disciplining children, but more especially trusting children and helping to teach them the responsibility that trust means—helping to teach them to make good decisions instead of scaring them to death. It is a long, tedious process, not greatly enhanced by critics who have made no effort to understand or to observe at firsthand.

Almost invariably the people who can't play it

straight make life very unpleasant for all of us. The sad thing is there are more and more such people. Stealing is a problem in boarding schools, increasingly so. It is a problem in day schools too, and private clubs and churches and business offices—law offices too, I'm told, and heaven knows in stores and on the streets. Lying, cheating, stealing, drinking are not new to any campus. They were not invented by this generation of students. What is new is the growing comfortable conviction of parents and students alike that lying, cheating, and stealing are just a normal stage in the adolescent growth process. "So what's the big deal?"

A mother whose fifteen-year-old daughter I suspended for two weeks for leaving her hotel room late at night during a school-sponsored trip and going down to the bar for a drink said, "You're making such a big deal of it. Frankly, I'm rather pleased. I didn't think she had the guts." A father who wrote, "Right on! I support you completely," in answer to a letter I had sent to parents about liquor and drugs behaved unspeakably less than three weeks later when his daughter was expelled for a drug related offense.

On one of the nights, when the students and I sat around munching cookies and chatting, we discussed whether or not a student council member who had broken a major rule should automatically go off the council. To me the answer was quite obvious, but the girls themselves expressed grave reservations. A very popular member of the council had just broken a major rule and I had insisted that she step down immediately. They disapproved of my action because the student in question was a fine girl who happened to make a hasty and very bad decision and knew beyond a shadow of a doubt that she had done so.

The question arose, "Should student council mem-

179

bers, given as they are a great deal of responsibility at Madeira, be asked to take a simple oath to uphold the school's rules?" We talked until late that night and the girls left with no decision made, still asking why a student council member should get any more punishment than any other student—that is, the regular punishment, plus dismissal from the council. There were three more meetings about it before they could honestly see the equity of it.

There was a bad storm during one of our meetings and one of the mothers who didn't want to drive back home in the rain had been invited by me to stay and have dinner and spend the night at my house, called "The Hill." She sat there listening to the girls that evening and said after they had left, "If I hadn't heard that conversation I wouldn't believe it ever took place. They really seem to have no convictions about right and wrong. It's all relative."

It was true. But it's true of our whole society and we criticize it most in the young—the ones who learned it from us. Less than a month before I left Madeira for good, the daughter of that woman did something seriously dangerous, to her own safety and to that of others as well. Her mother was on the phone until after 1:00 A.M. protesting vehemently and angrily about the punishment she was about to receive—a few days' suspension.

Hardest of all—I guess it's everyone's problem today—was finding time to think, and people who wanted to think with me. I wanted to think about education and the needs of students and how both can best be served. I wanted to evaluate what we were doing and how we could do it better, especially in the light of swiftly changing times. In almost three years at Madeira I had exactly one quiet, pleasant discussion with one of the twenty board members about education and its place in the lives, the unspeakably complicated lives, of young women today. The word came back so often that "board meetings are boring!" It came to seem almost a waste of time to write a report for them.

In a report written for the school by Russell Browning Associates, a board member was quoted as saying, "Mrs. Harris thinks with her mouth." I was hurt and shocked by the rudeness, but a case can be made for doing just that. Useful thoughts do occur to intelligent people as they share ideas.

Browning's report, requested at great expense by the board of directors to evaluate the school's position before embarking on a large fund-raising drive, turned out to be a long mishmash of rumors and quotes with none of the sources named. In it, both the board and the headmistress were labeled inadequate.

One director expressed serious doubts about Mrs. Harris and felt the headmistress was "irrational, at least she acts as if she is." Another member felt the board should admit they had made a mistake in hiring Mrs. Harris and see that she leave Madeira "quickly and as nicely as possible." The board was then advised to hire an interim head and form a new search committee which would be more "thoughtful."

Rarely had the head of a school become such a controversial figure in such a short time, and never had the head been less aware of it. I knew that the board should be helping me more than it was, and I knew that many of its members were obviously bored during board meetings, but I kept plunging ahead, eager beaver that I was.

On seeing the report, I was devastated, yet I appreciated the chairman's decency in showing it to me. I had worked very hard and the good results were beginning to show. There had been not one suggestion made to me in two years that the board had any questions about my competency, or that they questioned the efficacy of my efforts in the school's behalf. They just sat around at parties and discussed it. Fewer than a third of them had ever called and asked to help me in any way. I had entertained all of them at my own expense. About half of them had invited me to their homes, or bothered to take me out to lunch.

The total contribution of one of the male members of the board was to drop by occasionally and tell us how important he was, and whatever our problems might be he had connections that would set them all right again. As it turned out, he was one of the main causes of the biggest problem.

I showed Hy the report, and discussed briefly with him whether or not I should stay or leave Madeira. His comment didn't make me feel any better: "Hell, they won't fire you. They don't want the trouble of looking for someone else."

When it was released, the report caused an instant furor, and it left me totally sick at heart. Nothing had prepared me for anything so casually, irresponsibly cruel. An immediate vote was taken, unbeknownst to me, by telephone, to decide whether I stayed or went. One board member told me, "There was just one vote against you." Later, another member of the board smiled a nasty little smile and said, "Congratulations. You won by one vote." To this day I have no idea which one was telling the truth. By not knowing it drew the iron curtain down all the more firmly between me and Madeira. There was now no one to trust.

182

The classic symptoms of depression that I had felt and fought for a long time were finally overwhelming me. That exhaustion is a symptom of depression hadn't occured to me and certainly Hy didn't suggest it. I thought it was just long hours and seven day work weeks. Hy reminded me a little of my mother— a good, practicing Christian Scientist who saw all four of her children through everything from mumps and measles to whooping cough and scarlet fever with a big smile, a bowl of barley soup, and the warm assurance that, "You'll be fine tomorrow, honey."

Hy would say, "God, you've got it all. You're so lucky. Stop complaining. You ought to spend a few days doing rounds with me, and you'd count your blessings."

A few months before his death he said, "I'm going to make you spend a day in a nursing home some time and you'd stop complaining about how you feel."

I liked having him talk to me that way. I thought it was just what I needed. Toughen up, lady, and count your blessings. The formula worked for fifty-six years.

I had been checked for thyroid deficiency a number of times, even for ulcers, and told I was in tip-top condition. I was taking vitamin B shots, lots of vitamins, and eating candy bars by the dozen because I thought they made me feel peppier. I had started taking Desoxyn in small quantities years before. Hy prescribed it. I had said to him so many times, "I know how to do it, Hy. I know what is needed but I'm afraid I'll run out of strength."

The challenge of the job, the pleasure of working with bright people and new ideas, the driving desire to help young women grow up better prepared for life than I was, thinking ahead, growing strong without so many scars—these kept me motivated and moving. And occasional weekends with Hy helped me refuel when I had given all of me there was. Unfortunately, the more of me I gave the less I could get away to see Hy.

There were Fridays when I arrived at Purchase just about able to crawl over the threshold on my hands and knees, totally spent. By Sunday I was alive again. Much of the weekend I spent alone, reading, sunning, working my way through a briefcase of letters and reports, but doing it in an unhurried way, not running in to defrost the refrigerator, answer the phone, be Adult-on-Duty, or polish silver for another mothers' coffee. Hy would be at the office in the morning and, depending on the time of year, go hunting, play golf, or get into a gin game in the afternoon. My being there didn't change his pattern in any way, but it did mine. I was at peace there.

It says something sad about all of our society that the moment Hy died so many people were comfortable with the "murder of passion" explanation for his death . . . the jealous woman scorned, and we all know what "hell hath no fury like." The fact that I had moved to Virginia three years before, that Dr. Tarnower's affair with "the other woman" was at least ten years old, and that during that ten years and before, there had been a number of other women, including two he thought he would marry, are all simple facts they don't want to confuse their prejudices with. The fact that Mrs. Harris was exhausted and depressed, holding down a back-breaking job while her relationship with the people who were meant to help and support her, the Madeira board of directors, was shaky at best and openly hostile in some cases, did not appear in any newspaper. It isn't sexy or lurid, or even simple.

Suicide was not a new idea to me. It had been somewhere in the back of my mind for many years, the final steam valve, the final option. I don't fully understand why, but I had spent many years contemplating death, not in a morbid way, but as the final place to run to when I wasn't competent enough to go on living.

I have felt for many years that my depression was a chemical thing in my brain, something over which I had no control, the same thing that had destroyed my father's life, and caused an uncle to commit suicide. How the medication that Hy had given me for ten years affected the final explosion in my brain I cannot say.

The day I bought a gun in Virginia was not the first time I had tried to buy one. The first time was down in Florida in 1974, when Hy and I were in Palm Beach. Hy was playing golf and I spent a day driving around trying to find a gun. When I finally found one small enough for my hands they wouldn't sell it to me because I didn't have a Florida driver's license. Then, when I tried to find my way back to LaCoquille Club I was hopelessly lost. I got back just as Hy returned from eighteen holes of golf. He never knew, or had any idea how I had spent the day. There was so much we didn't know about one another. Perhaps it was inevitable that we would spend that last tragic night together as total strangers.

My own strong conviction is that I would have resorted to suicide long before if Hy hadn't been there saying "Welcome home, darling," and teaching me how to enjoy life, or at least letting me watch him enjoy it. Being put down was old stuff to me. My father's idea of the lowliest of human endeavors was teaching, and he rarely missed an opportunity to say

185

so. Then he would stop short and look as though it had just slipped his mind that I had been teaching for twenty or thirty years.

Hy seemed to respect what I did, and what I was. He is the only man who ever made me realize that being a woman can be a good thing to be. Alone with him I felt elevated for many years to the dignity of being a person. At parties I usually slipped back into feeling like a faceless "girl friend." At parties, away from Hy, I was simply the extra woman, the headmistress, the extension of a desk that walked and talked.

Part of my depression over the years had grown from the constant reminders that for all the honest to God giving of myself that I did, I was a nonperson in large parts of my private and professional life. To the faculty and students I was real as long as school was in session. To the members of the board I was a little like "the sad nervous boys in a Strindberg book—well fed, well groomed, well cared for but unacknowledged as a fellow human being." To Hy's friends, the four closest whom we saw constantly, I was a warm body, an interchangeable part, taking up space at the table. When Arthur Schulte, Hy's closest friend, wanted a gin game, which was all the time, he didn't care if the woman sitting quietly in the background was the "socialite headmistress of the Madeira School" or the madame of a local whorehouse. His wife Vivian did, but not Arthur.

The newspapers referred to me as "Dr. Tarnower's girlfriend," an opprobrium I despise. Oddly enough Dr. Tarnower was never referred to as "Mrs. Harris's boyfriend" or even "Her aging lover." The feminists still have their work cut out for them.

In the end, I had become a nonperson to Hy too, or perhaps I now had to admit what had always been true. From 1971 on, Mrs. Tryforos's letters, phone calls, telegrams, cute little gifts had never stopped following us around the world in our travels. Just before Hy died we spent Christmas together down in Palm Beach. We were there for two very happy weeks. Mrs. Tryforos outdid herself this time. In addition to phone calls and telegrams, she placed an ad on the front page of *The New York Times* to tell the doctor, long distance, that she loved him forever. It was something that might be considered "cute" if you could spare the $250 that it cost, if you were in your teens, and if the person you addressed it to wasn't a sixty-nine-year-old man spending a two week vacation with another woman. Under the circumstances it would be hard to imagine anything more tasteless and deliberately mean.

Hy looked at it in horror. "Jesus!" he said. "I hope none of my friends see it."

I should have said. "I'm your friend, Hy, and I see it." But the habit to laugh off hurt was too ingrown by then. "Why don't you have her try the Goodyear blimp next time, Herm?" I asked.

A woman simply wasn't a man's friend in Hy's world, no matter how she had been tested, and God knows I had been tested. She was something men had on the side—in addition to friends.

I believe the sad truth is that Hy was incapable of loving a woman, though he wanted desperately to be able to. He worked at it assiduously, and he was never happier than during those brief periods when he thought he had succeeded. How very sad that I know him better now than I did while he was alive.

Hy was never a complainer, but far more than his back and his stomach hurt him from time to time, and one enduring hurt lasted all his life. Hy prized money and social respectability as perhaps only a bright, ambitious, poor Jewish boy can. But social acceptance in his lifetime, and in spite of all the protests, even now, require men to make love to women, not to other men. Hy worked at it overtime, a girl here, a woman there, a chippie here, a rich widow there, a whole goyim beanery of them. He made a lifetime job of trying to prove to himself and others that he was in every sense of the word eminently male, and therefore eminently respectable.

But treating women badly, putting them down, was a physical necessity for him. He disliked them. He spent a lifetime collecting them and throwing them away. He said to me many times, with deep feeling, "There is no way you can know another person's suffering, Jean." And each time I thought he was talking about his patients.

Hy was a master of the game of one-upmanship. If the rules of the game said a bachelor was supposed to have women, then by God he'd have them. He fought what I think God made him every step of the way. But the closest he came to honest-to-God love was in his relationship with other men. I have no way of knowing whether those relationships were sexual. He often talked around the subject with me, how the ancient Greeks and Romans were considered quite respectable if they had young boys as companions. The only reason Hy ever gave me for breaking our engagement was, "I'm afraid, Jean. I'm afraid of the boys." I thought he meant they might be too noisy. Maybe he did. If I had had daughters he'd have found another reason.

At least one of Hy's closest friends felt as he did, used women but loved men. I rather imagine their relationship from beginning to end could have been photographed for family time on TV, but they loved one another more than they loved women. Two bright, rich, ambitious old men, yet burdened with

188

loving one another, burdened and comforted.

It was probably harder for men Hy's age to face this in themselves, but easier to pass socially, since women, in their generational myths, were not too bright, not too able, not even too stable, but merely decorative and functional. You could sneer at them more easily and still be socially attractive.

One of Hy's closest friends said to me once, "Hy loves to put you down. Why do you stand for it?"

It really didn't matter to me. I had always found putdowns a much more endearing sign of friendship than flattery. There were so many strengths in Hy to love. For his sake I was sorry about the weaknesses, but they weren't important to me in any other way.

Hy was the only man I ever loved. I respected the many good things about him, and was proud of his competence. He gave me more solace than I gave him because I obviously needed more—or I couldn't find it in as many places as he could. But I led a very full life away from him, full of family and hard work with few illusions about him sitting alone for months at a time when I couldn't see him.

One summer an old friend of Hy's greeted me on the terrace of his club with, "How grand to see you. I thought Hy was just seeing that Lynne person now." It had come out too fast and she looked embarrassed.

"Oh, Margaret," I said, "Hy has always had other women. It's nothing new."

Later I hold Hy about it. He laughed heartily. "Is that what you told her? Good for you! It was just the right thing to say."

In 1977 before I moved to Virginia we were reaching a fork in the road. I would be working, and working hard for another two years. Hy was slowing down, professionally. I don't think he would ever have retired, but vacations were becoming more and more

189

frequent, "and I won't travel alone, Jean." He even talked about buying a home in Florida. Happy incidents of geography and timing had made it possible for us to pursue our professional lives to the fullest and still see one another often. It would never be possible again. I wrote him a long, earnest letter about our friendship, and we both vowed we would always touch base when we could.

The word "earnest" makes me smile and think of a satire about "earnest" women that Nora Ephron wrote recently. We should always be done in satire.

I wrote him that summer about my busy life and my hopes for the school and ended:

> Since the moment I met you I have made my own life. I go on making my own life and by and large it's as interesting as the next, more so I suppose—but that doesn't replace the knowledge that somewhere at the other end of a phone, or a plane ride, or a damned long drive you are sitting there alive, well, self-contained, bright, interesting, quite smug about how well you have planned your life, aggravating, remarkably cruel at times, unbelievably kind at others. And nothing and no one can replace the gladness I feel that you are there.

In spite of all my brave plans for Madeira I was obviously lonely—loneliness is something most of us live with, and I'm sure people die of it too. But it was the belief, one I still hold, that I no longer had the strength to perform my life's work, that made me finally truly suicidal. Where the strength had gone, whether it had been honestly used to the last full measure, or dissipated in unproductive ways, is of little consequence now. I only know it was gone.

I had spent a long weekend with Hy three weeks before he died. He gave the rehearsal dinner for my son David's wedding. He was funny and kind and warm and passionate, the closest thing to loving he knew how to be. We sat on his bed that Sunday morning before I left. I thanked him for all he had done and said to him, "You don't act like a man who's in love with another woman. But then you never have."

"You of all people should know better than that," he said. "I don't love anyone, and I don't need anyone."

It isn't a message to gladden the heart—quite the opposite—but it was old news to me by now.

I knew Hy as well as anyone could know him. I told him I was appalled to hear that he was thinking of taking someone else to a dinner given by the Westchester Heart Association in his honor. It was the culmination of his medical career and I expected to be there to honor him.

He said the predictable, "Look—it isn't that important," and then added, "She's done a lot of work for the Association."

"She should, Herm. She's a paid employee of yours."

He smiled, uncomfortably. "I know. I guess you're right."

I told him I would be in New York anyway on April 18 to be part of a seminar at Columbia University.

"Fine," he said.

We would make it a weekend in Purchase. He kissed me goodbye and I headed back to Virginia.

Besides the memory of a lovely weekend I carried with me his rough draft of what was to be the first chapter of his new book. He asked me to write into it some changes and suggestions I had made that weekend. His version and mine were both terrible, but he thanked me enthusiastically when I returned it rewritten a few days later. Assistant District Attorney George Bolen was to tell the jury, "She stole it. He didn't give it to her."

As I left the house and headed up Purchase Street I remembered that I wanted to call Dan Comfort, a friend of Hy's who was instrumental in planning the dinner, and tell him all was well for the nineteenth. I had called him a few weeks before because Hy had been ambivalent about that weekend. I had said my goodbyes and didn't want to go back to Hy's house, so I stopped at the public phone at the old post office. It was the same place I would head three weeks later seeking help for Hy when his phone was dead.

I was deeply hurt that Hy would play games about something as important as the dinner, that he could be so insensitive to an old friend. Our relationship was different now, but I was, what I would always be, a loving friend, and I expected to be treated as one. My overreaction to everything Dan had said three weeks before should have been a signal to both Dan and me that I was cracking up. Dan had invited me to sit at his table, which was kind of him, though he obviously wished I were burdening someone else with the call. Now I called him from the post office phone, told him what a great weekend we had just had, and assured him I would see him on the nineteenth.

I had long since had every reason to be disillusioned with Hy, his obsession with self, his insensitivity. I knew that distance had changed our life together and that his new life-style, with quite different people now kowtowing to a "bestseller," required someone on call, someone able to pick up and travel whenever he whistled. He was another man now, and it was well that I didn't see him too often—that way I could cling more easily to the memory of the old one. I knew that I would never love anyone else.

Too many lovely memories had woven a knot that no one would ever unravel. I knew that I would always be alone and that over the long haul hard work would be the only "lasting relationship" for me. Perhaps that's why it went on being important to me that someone strong, whatever the source of his strength, be there to touch base with. I didn't admire Hy's morality, once I discovered what it was, but I admired his strength and I wished that I had it. I thought the buffeting I took from him was the best thing in the world for me. For some perverse reason I never stopped feeling safe with Hy. Away from him I was more vulnerable. In the end, if he had lived in California I would have made my way to see him before I died.

I had started that Monday morning by mailing a letter to him, feeling deeply depressed. Vacations were particularly enormous. I dreaded them. Suddenly the campus was so quiet and empty. The reason for being there left when the girls left, and I hated the loneliness of three weeks on those four hundred acres and the terrifying prospect of time to think about me. The letter was a long, confused, bitter polemic written that weekend in response to a phone conversation I had had with him on Thursday at the height of the handwringing and soul-searching about expulsion of four of the seniors. I sent the letter by registered mail because so many things I had sent him in the past three years had mysteriously never arrived—not even a telegram that Western Union records show was delivered, not even the invitation to David's wedding.

As soon as I had mailed it I was sorry. It would make him cross because it wasn't the usual happy, funny stuff I usually ground out. It was an anguished wail, held back for many years. A few moments later my own mail arrived with a letter from one of the students about the recent expulsion. It was that one rotten, extra straw — the coup de grace, the culmination of almost three years of hard work, loneliness, and trauma. My reaction to the letter was out of proportion to the letter itself, but not for me at the moment. It was annihilating. I sat through the day's appointments trying to listen and respond. At 3:30 P.M. I said to be secretary, "Please cancel the next appointment. I've had enough, Carol. I'm going home."

I walked back to The Hill, the house I lived in on the Madeira campus, and rewrote my will. I had it witnessed by three ladies in the office, and wrote notes to my sister Mary Margaret, my secretary Carol, and to the chairman of the board. No one questioned the will. I was distraught but somehow no one knew. My mind was a shambles but my house was in order. There was only one thing I wanted to do—see Hy for a few moments, just chat with him one more time, and then go down to the pond, to the right of it where the weeping willow used to be and so many daffodils bloom in the spring, and kill myself. I began to feel as anxious for death as I had once felt anxious to see Hy, that feeling of urgency and exhilaration each time I turned in the driveway at Purchase.

I called Hy about 4:15 P.M. to say I was coming—not why. Henri, Hy's chauffeur, answered the phone. He said Hy was out and was going out to dinner. I said I'd call back. I had called Hy off and on all weekend as I had felt myself crumbling away. But he was always out and Henri or Suzanne, Henri's wife and Hy's housekeeper, answered instead. Suzanne

194

had heard the anguish in my voice and said, "Are you all right, madame?" and I had said, "Oh, no, Suzanne, I'm not. I'm not all right at all." But it wasn't her problem.

At 5:15 P.M. I called again and Hy answered. I said, "Darling, I'd like to come and talk with you for a little while tonight."

He said, "Well, Debby's coming for dinner." Debby was Hy's favorite niece. Even at that point he couldn't say "Debby and Lynne."

"That doesn't matter. She always leaves early and it will be almost 11:00 before I get there," I replied.

"It's more convenient if you come tomorrow."

"I can't talk with you tomorrow, Hy. Please just this once, let me say when."

"Suit yourself," he answered. I told him I would leave right away and we hung up.

What a sad little line that was, "Please, just this once let me say when." It sounded like Lynne Tryforos years before when she kept coming to the house while I was there, never venturing inside but spending many hours outside.

I had said to her finally, "Lynne, does it not seem bizarre to you that you are here when I am here?"

She looked puzzled.

"Lynne," I repeated, "why are you here?"

"I'm here because I'm allowed to be," she answered in a pouty, little girl voice.

It seemed a pathetic, sad answer to me then. It seems the more so to me today as I finally accept the reality that that was why anyone was there, including me. I thought for years it was a sign of his total disrespect and disregard for the woman that he would permit her to come to the house while I was there as long as she didn't come inside. Imagine such hubris and worse such naiveté in a grown woman. It is only

195

since Hy's death, since I have started writing, that I have faced all these simple truths.

Pity me that the heart is slow to learn
What the swift mind beholds at every turn.

"The Harp Weaver"
Edna St. Vincent Millay

I took the gun out of the closet and out onto the terrace and shot it into the air. I had put two bullets in the gun, pulled the trigger, expecting the relief of an explosion, but it had only clicked and clicked again. Finally it fired. "Dear God," I thought, "I don't want that to happen tonight. This is suicide, not Russian roulette."

I took out a small handful of bullets and put them in my pocket while I tried to pry out the empty shells. (I didn't know until months later, when my lawyer Joel Aurnou showed me, that a simple press of a rod in the cartridge would have emptied it. Had I known that much about the gun I would have died before Hy did.) The shells wouldn't budge. I took the gun into the kitchen, opened the drawer where the ice pick was, and poked out the shells. I was hurrying now. I filled the cartridge with bullets, or thought I did. It was five months after Hy's death before I learned that I had put only five bullets in. One space in the cartridge was empty.

I put the gun in my handbag, propped the three notes and an envelope filled with all the papers David and Jim would need on a chair in the hall, hugged Cider, the big golden retriever the Madeira girls had given me, and Liza, the little springer spaniel David and Jim gave to me, and went out to the car.

As I opened the car door I saw a bouquet of flowers

on the front seat. A teacher who had seen me read the student's letter that morning, and who had watched the mounting trauma all week, had brought them to me with a note that read:

Monday, March 10
I believe in mythical renewal—the resurrection of the spirit—yours, mine, and that of the un--predictable young!

Love,
Ruth

Not wanting to disturb me by ringing the bell, she left them on the seat of the car. I wish she had rung the bell. I wonder if I would have run a comb quickly through my hair and answered the door as though nothing were wrong, or thrown myself into her arms and wept.

I had been screaming for help for years but somehow whatever came out never rang true, or never sounded important enough to take seriously. I had said to Miss Florence, my history teacher at Laurel, that I had doubts about myself heading off to college. "You—doubting yourself? You'll thrive there. You always do." That was the stock answer. Years later, after my divorce, when life was proving more than I could understand or cope with, I cried "Help" in earnest.

I turned to the minister at Christ Church—or tried to. I called him three different times, told him a little and asked to see him. I guess I picked bad times — he had more trauma than he could handle then. He never called back, and he never came to call. Finally one night after the boys were in bed I stood on the landing of the stairway and quietly and deliberately tore off my skirt and blouse and ripped them into a hundred small pieces. It was like lancing a boil. It helped. Then, having humiliated myself with this mindless self-indulgence, I picked up the pieces, threw them away and set about the business of being a conscientious mother and teacher again.

In Philadelphia we lived three blocks from church. The boys and I went every Sunday; Jimmy was confirmed there—Hy was there that day. One Sunday afternoon when the accumulation of exhaustion and despair had me wondering if I should be in a hospital I called the minister and asked him if I could come see him. It wasn't convenient, but I begged and he said, "Very well—come along." I stayed for two hours sobbing out my sad little sadnesses. He gave me a cup of tea, patted my shoulder sympathetically, and sent me home. We stayed in Philadelphia another year after that visit. The minister didn't call, but he smiled warmly on Sunday mornings. The day the moving van was moving us to Connecticut he walked by the house and waved, and asked where I was going.

While we lived in Connecticut and New York, from 1971 to August 1977, Hy was my sounding board, my oasis, my warm and reassuring friend. That's not to say I was constantly wringing my hands, weeping, and saying, "Help me." Quite the contrary. I was jovial, happy company. Touching base with Hy gave me a feeling of safety and stability so I could cope with whatever traumas life tossed my way. It was after I had been at Madeira for several months and was visiting Hy that I called a young psychiatrist in Connecticut. He had worked wonders for several students at the Thomas School and I was ready for a small wonder myself. I cared deeply about Madeira and about doing a good job there. It is a fine school and nothing I write should ever give the impression that I doubt or question that. But I assumed too much about it when I took the position and the board was never honest with me, so a job which under the best of circumstances is tough became backbreaking and heartbreaking.

The young psychiatrist was warm and friendly on the phone but I couldn't bring myself to say why I had called. I didn't really know what to say—and anyway when I talked about myself I always wept, which disgusted me, so I said a friendly "Hi and goodbye." I had heard so much from Hy about female patients with nameless symptoms who thought they were sick when they were just bored or lonely or self-indulgent, and I didn't want to be one of them.

"To hell with it," I decided. "There's nothing wrong with me I can't handle myself." I sublimated; I made a joke of it; I bought a mink hat; I told myself I was lucky and whatever it was that hurt didn't matter—and a few months later I bought my security blanket, a .32-caliber gun, and I comforted myself with the knowledge that if the pain of living grew unbearable I could use the gun—on me. That is the only use it was ever meant for.

I have spent a lifetime trying to make myself believe that I mattered enough to go on living. I think I did believe it when I decided on suicide, but I had run out of energy by then and I knew I no longer had the heart or the physical strength to go on functioning in a useful way.

Did I say "decided"? It's the wrong word. You don't sit down and list the pros and cons. It becomes your only option—even more, it becomes a physical need. The plug was pulled and the only thing I wanted more than a quick, clean ending was to see Hy one more time before I went, and to die there by the pond at the place I loved, a place that had been home for me for almost nine years.

I had no thought of hurting Hy or telling him that I intended suicide. I had no intention of letting him see the gun. He was my last stop: I wouldn't keep him long. I didn't for a moment think it was an unfair or unreasonable request. It would be a nuisance getting rid of the body the next morning, but doctors are used to things like that. And Hy had said it himself many times, "I don't love anyone. I don't need anyone." He would have been sorry. But it wouldn't have ruined his day.

Harrison, New York:
The End of the Line

1.

It began to rain about an hour after I had left Madeira. The last thing I saw as I drove out the long, lovely drive was the bright smiling face of Kathleen Kavanaugh out walking her little dog, "Killer." How ugly innocent things sound now. "I could kill that boy for leaving his room like this!" I must have said it many many times. "People who dump their beer and liquor bottles around this beautiful pond should be shot." I said it one day months after Hy died and then froze. "My God—what if Jim Ferron—heard me. He walks by the same pond and writes for *The New York Times*. Proof positive—I heard it. She's a killer!"

The drive was a strangely peaceful and mindless one. The decision to kill myself was so firmly made it was comforting. No more endless sleepless nights, no more ugly phone calls in the night, no more fighting each step of the way, usually about things you shouldn't have to mention twice; no more ugly conversations with my father about my children, my two very decent sons; no more watching grown men and women on a board of directors making poor decisions to mollify other members of the board who cared more about their memory of Madeira, than Madeira as it should be today. No more imposing on Hy for comfort, when turning seventy depressed and frightened him and he was settling into his own kind of comfort.

I walked into the house on Purchase Street that night as I had for fourteen years, full of love and happy to be there. I expected to be dead within the hour. Hy hadn't left a light on though he knew I was coming. It was pitch black and raining, and I stumbled on the stair. But I was relieved to be there. I felt safer than I had all day.

The story of what happened in Hy's bedroom on the night of March 10, 1980, is one I have told again and again to the very best of my ability. I have told it to doctors, lawyers, and family and friends. Had I been given another trial I would have told the same story again. The truth doesn't change.

What follows is taken directly from the public record of my trial. It never for a moment occurred to me that I should not take the stand. I am the only person alive who knows what happened that night. I had a moral obligation to Hy and to myself to take the stand and tell it. I believed it was the right thing to do then. I still believe it, although there were many who wrote later, "Mrs. Harris convicted herself. The jury didn't think she proved her innocence."

I took the stand on January 27, 1981, the thirty-eighth day of the trial, and was questioned for the next nine days. Having first identified myself I was asked to identify the papers I had left propped up on chairs in the front hall at Madeira: my will, insurance papers, and letters to the chairman of the board, my secretary, and my sister Mary Margaret. The letter to the chairman had been prompted by the Browning report, and by a letter I had received that morning saying I shouldn't have expelled four girls because "lots of other girls are doing the same thing. You don't know what is going on."

Joel Aurnou read my letter to the board chairman to the jury.

Dear Alice,

I'm sorry. Please for Christ's sake don't open again until you have adults and policemen and keepers on every floor. God knows what they're doing. And next time, choose a head the board wants and supports. Don't let some poor fool work like hell for two years before she knows she wasn't wanted in the first place.

At this point Assistant District Attorney Bolen objected and said, "Can we establish when these comments were made, if at all, in relation to March 10, 1980, especially when this document was purportedly written?"

The letter had already been turned over by the chairman of the board and sworn to by her as having been found in the front hall of the house I lived in at Madeira early in the morning of March 11, and was in evidence. But what did he care? The game of justice turns truth upside down.

The letter continued, "There are so many enemies, and so few friends. I was a person and no one ever knew." It took nine pages of testimony to get those six sentences out, with Bolen's constant objections, and the judge's repeated "Sustained." Finally, Joel asked:

Aurnou: On March 10, 1980—Jean, look at me please. When you wrote the words "I was a person and no one ever knew," tell the jury what you meant.

Harris: I don't know. I think it had something to do with being a woman who had worked a long time and had done the things a man does to support his family, but still a woman, and I always felt that when I was in Westchester I was a woman in a pretty dress and went to a dinner party with Dr. Tarnower, and in Washington I was a woman in a pretty dress and the headmistress, but I wasn't sure who I was, and it didn't seem to matter.

Aurnou: It mattered to you, didn't it?

Harris: I was a person sitting in an empty chair, Joel. I can't describe it anymore.

There was a brief recess and then the questioning went on.

Aurnou: When you went to Hy's, that trip took several hours?

Harris: Five hours.

Aurnou: Tell the jury, please, exactly how you felt, what you were thinking about during that trip, what emotional state you were in.

Harris: I can really only remember thinking two things. For about the first hour I felt as though I should call friends and tell them I wouldn't be there for dinner. They were having the first big dinner party since their marriage and I had been looking forward to it sort of, but I couldn't think of anything to say to them. I was afraid if I called them I'd burst into tears. So I kept thinking about it and it was on my conscience, but I didn't stop to call them to say I wouldn't be there. Then after it was late enough, it didn't make any difference. They already knew I wasn't going to be there. I really had a very peaceful, mindless kind of trip after that.

I felt at peace with the knowledge that I had finally come to the end of the road and dying didn't frighten me. Then, just as I came across the George Washington Bridge, I thought if I stayed too long—what if Hy said something that spoiled my resolve to die, and I brushed that aside very quickly, thinking I won't stay that long, I just want to see him for a little while and feel safe one more time, and I won't let him—I won't let him know what I am going to do and I won't let it spoil my resolve, and after that I just drove until I drove into his driveway.

Aurnou: And when you got to his driveway and drove up the driveway, will you tell us what you saw?

Harris: I saw a house that was very dark, and I felt just as good as I always did when I drove in that driveway.

Aurnou: But there were no lights on?

Harris: No, not a light. Not that I saw . . .

Aurnou: What did you do after you stopped the car?

Harris: I stopped right in front of the front steps and I was sort of surprised not to see a light on, but I thought, well, maybe he left the door ajar and didn't want to leave a light on. So I got out of the car and started up the steps, and then I remembered the flowers and I thought it would be nice to take him the flowers. So I went back and opened up the other side of the car and I reached in for the flowers and I had put them on top of my pocketbook and I picked up my pocketbook, too, and the flowers, and I closed the door and walked up the steps to the front door and it was locked.

Aurnou: When you went back and got the flowers, you also got your pocketbook at that time?

Harris: Yes. I just picked it up the way you would pick up your pocketbook. I hadn't left the driver's side with anything in my hand, but I did go back for the flowers and took my pocketbook, too.

Aurnou: When you picked up the flowers and picked up the pocketbook, where was the gun?

Harris: It was in the pocketbook.

Aurnou: What happened next?

Harris: I walked up the stairs and tried the door and it was locked. So I just walked back downstairs and went in the way we usually went in, anyway, which was through the garage. I opened the garage door on the right-hand side, the one where Henri and Suzanne had their car, and then I walked around in back of Hy's car and I pushed the button for his door in order to make the light go on, so I could see what I was doing, and then I walked up to the first floor, and it was all dark there and quiet, and I called to Hy from the bottom of the stairs and then walked upstairs.

Aurnou: What did you say when you called to Hy?

Harris: I just called, "Hy, Hy," and I walked upstairs and he was just beginning to stir when I got to the top of the stairs, and I walked over and sat—

Aurnou: Wait a minute. You got to the top of the stairs.

Harris: The first floor.

Aurnou: Now you got to the top of the stairs at some point on the second floor, did you not?

Harris: Yes.

Harris: Yes.

Aurnou: What did you have in your hands?

Harris: I had the flowers and my pocketbook.

Aurnou: What did you do?

Harris: I heard Hy just stirring and I walked over and sat on the edge of my bed and reached over and turned on the light, and the light over his bed went on.

Aurnou: First of all, Mrs. Harris, is that a dimmer switch?

Harris: No, it is not. It's just a switch that turns lights on or off.

Aurnou: Could you tell us how it works? Is it anything more than a click switch?

Harris: Yes. It's a nuisance. I think there are two parts to it and there are several different lights on the same connection. I have never seen anything quite like it, as a matter of fact. You turn this knob and push the switch and the light over Hy's bed would go on, and then you turn it again and push the switch again and the light over the table would go on and you turn it again and push the switch and the light over my bed would go on. But they were either on or off. They couldn't make them darker, dimmer, or brighter.

Aurnou: In other words, whatever position the switch was in would control which lights went on?

Harris: That's right.

Aurnou: But whichever light went on went on in one intensity; it was not a matter of a dimmer switch?

Harris: That's right.

Aurnou: When you actually pressed it that night when you came in and sat down on your bed, which light or lights was it that went on?

Harris: I didn't turn the switch. I just pushed the thing and I guess the last thing to go off was the light over Hy's bed, so that's what went back on again.

Aurnou: What did you do next?

Harris: Well Hy was just waking up and rubbing his eyes and I said, "Hi. I thought you would leave a lamp in the window, it's black as pitch out there," and he was not enthralled to see me and he said, "Jesus, it's the middle of the night," waking up (indicating), and I said, "It's not really that late and I'm not going to stay very long. I just came for a while to talk with you," and he said, "Well, I'm not going to talk to anybody in the middle of the night," and he turned toward me.

He always had two pillows on his bed and he was lying on one and hugging the other one and he said, "I don't feel like talking in the middle of the night," and he closed his eyes. So I sat for a minute thinking he would wake up. He usually woke up very quickly, because he was used to phone calls in the middle of the night and getting up and getting dressed and racing out to a patient very fast, but he didn't seem inclined to wake up fast that night, and I finally said, "I brought you some flowers."

He didn't answer. And I said, after I waited a little while, "Have you written any more on the book?" and he said, "Jesus, Jean, shut up and go to bed," and I said, "I can't go to bed, dear, I'm not going to stay that long, I'm just going to be a little while," and I sat a while longer and he lay there hugging the pillow with his eyes closed, and I finally said, "Won't you really talk to me for just a little while?" and he didn't answer, and I sat some more, and finally I said—I didn't want to leave yet.

I was sure he would wake up and stick the other pillow in back of his head and say, "You're some kind of a nut to drive five hours in the middle of the night to talk, but what do you want to talk about?" So I was just kind of waiting.

And finally I said, "There is a shawl here, I want to be sure Kathleen has it, I'll just get it." I had given her a white shawl that she seemed very pleased with and I had a pretty black shawl somewhere in the drawer where I kept things.

Aurnou: Where was the shawl?

Harris: It was in the drawer in Hy's dresser that he had given to me where I would keep things over the years.

Aurnou: What if anything did you do then?

Harris: I got up and went around and opened up

the drawer and I saw the shawl. It was on the bottom of a lot of other things.

Aurnou: Someone has described a drawer back in the dressing room area as being open in this area. Was the drawer to which you went for the shawl in that general area?

Harris: Yes. It was that drawer. It wasn't open when I went there. I opened it.

Aurnou: Before you opened it, did you do anything in that area?

Harris: Yes. I turned on the light so I could see. There is a light switch almost above where the cross is that was supposed to be where the drawer was. That was the one switch I used the most because it didn't have one of those turning dials on. It was just an ordinary switch. So a lot of time when I went up there in the dark I went around and turned on the dressing room light instead of fussing with the one in between the beds. Anyway, I turned that on so I could see what I was doing.

Aurnou: When you were doing that, where were the flowers?

Harris: On the bed where I had put them.

Aurnou: Which bed?

Harris: On my bed. I sat down. My pocketbook went to the left of me and the flowers went to the right of me. Hy was not enthralled by the gift of flowers. He wanted sleep.

Aurnou: Where was your pocketbook when you went back to get the shawl?

Harris: Right where it had been, on the side of— should I show you there?

Aurnou: No. Just tell us which location it was in.

Harris: If you were sitting facing Hy on my bed, it was on my left, near the foot of the bed, and the flowers were near the pillow. I think they were on the pillow.

Aurnou: And you went back to get the shawl and what happened?

Harris: I pulled out the shawl and I think I pulled out a couple of other things with it. I am not really sure. I don't remember what I brought with it . . . I walked around and put them on the bed and looked at Hy and he still had his eyes closed, though I think by then he was wide awake, and then I turned back and went into the bathroom. I turned on the bathroom light.

Aurnou: Which bathroom did you turn the light on?

Harris: The one on the—

Aurnou: The one with the bathtub or the one with the shower?

Harris: The one I always used, nearest the bed. The one on the right-hand side.

The Court: Is that the one with the tub or the shower?

Harris: The tub. That's the one with the tub. And I turned on the light and I saw a number of things in the bathroom, one of them a negligee, a greenish blue satin negligee.

Aurnou: Was it yours?

Harris: No. And I looked at it, and having believed for a year that some things of mine had been destroyed by the owner of the negligee, I picked it up—I didn't pick it up. I took it off—

Bolen: Your honor, I ask that be stricken.

Harris: That was my reason.

The Court: I will sustain an objection. The last portion of the answer will be stricken, as to what somebody else may have done to her garment in the past. That item will be disregarded, ladies and gentlemen. You can go to the point where you picked up the negligee that you saw.

Harris: I took it off the hook where it was hanging and I walked into Hy's room and threw it on the floor. And Hy was still paying no attention. I thought I saw the negligee land on the floor. I don't know. I went back in the bathroom. By this time I felt hurt and frustrated, because the script wasn't working out the way I expected it to. I had wanted to feel safe one more time and I thought it was a reasonable request, but it wasn't happening, and I walked back into the bathroom and I picked up a box of curlers and threw them. I didn't really know where they landed. I just threw them in the bathroom, and I heard the noise. They apparently broke a window, though I didn't know until many months later that they had broken a window, and as I walked out of the bathroom Hy was standing at the door and his arm swung out and he hit me across the face.

Aurnou: Just a minute, Mrs. Harris. You were in the bathroom when you threw the curlers?

Harris: Yes.

Aurnou: Where was the doctor at that time?

Harris: He was in his bed.

Aurnou: Did you actually see him get out of bed?

Harris: No, I didn't see him until I walked out. I didn't really see him even, I just felt him.

Aurnou: You said that you came out of the bathroom, your bathroom, and the doctor was there and he swung and he struck you. Where?

Harris: Just across the face (indicating).

Aurnou: Had he ever done that before?

Harris: No, indeed, he never had. But then I had never come to his house and thrown something before, either.

Aurnou: Well, let's talk about that. When you drove from Virginia to Purchase, did you ever intend

211

anywhere along that trip before or during or right up to the moment you got there for Hy to kill you?

Harris: No, I certainly did not, and I am happy to finally be able to say it. It wouldn't have made any sense to get in a car and think I would drive there and hand a man like Hy a gun and ask him to kill me with it. He spent his life saving people's lives, besides which, I wouldn't have done that to him. I didn't want him to know what I was going to do. I had no intention of his ever seeing the gun or knowing anything about how desperate I was that night. I hoped it would be a quiet, pleasant, last few minutes.

Aurnou: And while we are back, was there anything unusual about the way you entered the house that night? Had you ever done that before?

Harris: That was the way we went in most of the time. The front door had no outside lock on it. If it was closed from the inside, the only way you could get it open was to ring the doorbell. The only time I ever rang the doorbell was when I saw Suzanne in the kitchen and knew she didn't have a long way to walk. Otherwise I always went down through the garage.

Aurnou: Now you are outside the bathroom and Hy has smacked you. What did you do?

Harris: My first reaction was to throw something else. So I turned around and went back in the bathroom and picked up something. I didn't know until I was told in this courtroom what it was. But I picked up a box and threw that, too. I threw that and it went into a cosmetic mirror of mine and smashed that and then scattered around on the floor.

Aurnou: Let me ask you this. After the second thing that you threw and the cosmetic mirror belonging to you shattered, where was Hy and what did Hy do?

Harris: He was standing right where I left him and

I walked back out and he did the same thing over again, exactly the same way, exactly the same spot. I made him very angry.

Aurnou: You told us originally that you went there because you felt safe and you wanted to have a quiet few minutes.

Harris: Yes.

Aurnou: What had you planned to do after that?

Harris: I had planned to leave and go down near the pond and shoot myself.

Aurnou: And here was the doctor, he smacked you twice in the face—

Harris: But he didn't know what I was going to do, Joel.

Aurnou: But what did you do then?

Harris: I didn't have any desire to throw any more things. It just hadn't turned out the way I thought it would, and I simply wanted to get dying over with. The pleasant talk was not to be. So I calmed down and I walked in and I sat on the edge of my bed facing away from his and I put my hair behind my ears and I raised my face to him and I closed my eyes and said, "Hit me again, Hy, make it hard enough to kill," which I guess I told the policeman something about, and that's what started the stupid story that I had gone to Westchester to ask Hy to kill me. It was the furthest thing from my mind.

Aurnou: But you did say it, then?

Harris: Yes, I did say it.

Aurnou: And what if anything did Hy say or do?

Harris: He didn't say anything. He stopped in front of me for an instant, I guess. It was long enough, so I wondered how much it would hurt if he did it, but he didn't touch me again. He walked away, and it probably took a great deal of self-control, because I am sure he was very mad by then. But he

213

didn't hit me again. He didn't say anything. He just walked away around my bed and over to somewhere near his bed. I never really saw exactly where he was standing right at the moment, and it was very quiet, and I got up, I think to go, and I walked around the foot of the bed and I picked up my pocketbook and I felt the gun and I unzipped the bag and took out the gun and I said, "Never mind, I'll do it myself," and I raised it to my head and pulled the trigger at the instant that Hy came at me and grabbed the gun and pushed my hand away from my head and pushed it down, and I heard the gun explode. It was very loud. It seemed very loud, because I didn't think I'd hear it, and Hy jumped back and I jumped back and he held up his hand and it was bleeding and I could see the bullet hole in it and he said, "Jesus Christ, look what you did," and we both just stood there and looked at it. I think he was as appalled as I was. I wasn't aiming the gun at Hy and I didn't even know he was looking at me, but he moved very fast and he was the one who was shot, and he stood and looked at it—

Aurnou: Just a minute, Mrs. Harris. When that happened, did you intend to shoot or harm the doctor?

Harris: No. I didn't even know he was nearby. I didn't even know he was looking at me. But I know I was the one who fired the gun.

Aurnou: Was that the first shot fired in that room that night while you were there?

Harris: Yes, it was.

Aurnou: Do you have any doubt about that at all?

Harris: No, there isn't any doubt about that. I know that beyond a shadow of a doubt. That's where I was standing and that's what he did.

Aurnou: After he looked at his hand and said,

"Jesus Christ, look what you've done," what did he do next?

Harris: He sort of stared at the hand for a minute and then he turned and went into the bathroom, and I stood there for a little while. I didn't have, I don't think, exactly a normal reaction to it, because I couldn't believe it happened. Ordinarily if he sounded hoarse, I was upset if he didn't take a pill, but I didn't feel—I didn't rush to help him. I stood there and stared at him, and then I followed him into the bathroom, or I started following him into the bathroom.

Aurnou: What stopped you, if anything?

Harris: I got about halfway around Hy's bed and I suddenly realized that the gun was still in here, and if I went back and got it fast enough, I could shoot myself before Hy—I could hear the water running and I thought I could get it over with before he even came back into the room. So I didn't go all the way into the bathroom with him. I turned around and went back and I looked at the foot of the bed and I didn't see the gun and I looked in between the beds and I didn't see it, and I got down on my knees and looked under my bed and it was there, and I reached under to get it. I was on my knees, down low, and I pulled it out, and as I pulled it out, Hy came out of the bathroom—I didn't actually see him at that moment. I didn't realize what he was doing until I could feel him, and I think he just flew over the bottom of the bed and he grabbed my left arm and he held it very, very tightly, and it hurt, and it made me drop the gun.

Aurnou: I would like you to look at Exhibits C, D, and F in evidence.

Harris: Yes.

Aurnou: What part or portion of your body that

Hy touched at that time is visible, if any, in those pictures?

Harris: The upper part of my arm, from the elbow on up, is visible.

Aurnou: Did you at any time that night have occasion to suffer any other injury to that portion of your arm, other than the time that he grabbed it and squeezed it tightly while you were holding the gun?

Harris: No. He wasn't trying to hurt me. He was trying to make me drop the gun.

Aurnou: Did you?

Harris: Yes, I did.

Aurnou: What happened then?

Harris: He picked up the gun. He held on to my arm for a while and he picked up the gun and then he got up and walked over and sat on the edge of his bed next to the little ledge where the telephone was and the buzzer, and I was on my knees and I looked at him and he looked at me and I came over in front of him—I don't think I got all the way up. I was kneeling in front of him and he buzzed the buzzer. He buzzed it several times.

Aurnou: Which buzzer are you talking about now?

Harris: The buzzer that would ring in the kitchen to make Suzanne and Henri come.

Aurnou: When he did that, where if anywhere do you recall the gun being?

Harris: Hy had it in his hand.

Aurnou: Which hand?

Harris: In his right hand, because he was buzzing with his left hand. He was sitting—should I show?

Aurnou: You can.

(Harris leaves the stand.)

Harris: He was sitting on the edge of the bed here.

Aurnou: Talk a little louder while you are away

216

from the mike.

Harris: He was sitting on the edge here (indicating) and his left hand was pushing the buzzer and his right hand had the gun and he put it down on the bed and put his hand on the bed.

(Harris returns to stand.)

And I came over to him and I was on my knees. From the time he first buzzed the buzzer I was panicked, because I was afraid Henri and Suzanne would come running up the steps any minute, and I said, "Hy, please give me the gun, please give me the gun, or shoot me yourself, but for Christ's sake let me die," and he looked at me and said, "Jesus, you're crazy, get out of here," and he pushed me aside and he reached for the phone, because once you buzz the buzzer you have to pick up the phone and talk to someone on one of the other phones.

Aurnou: Why were you afraid that Henri and Suzanne might come up?

Harris: Because he buzzed for them.

Aurnou: But what if they did come up?

Harris: Well, then I didn't have a chance of getting the gun again. I didn't think I did, anyway, because Hy even with his injured hand was stronger than I was.

Aurnou: What was it you thought they would prevent you from doing?

Harris: I wanted to shoot myself, Joel, and I was doing it in the wrong place.

Aurnou: After Hy buzzed the buzzer for the servant and picked up the phone with his left hand while you were kneeling in front of him, what happened next?

Harris: I pulled myself up on his knees, as a matter of fact, just holding onto them, and I was just about straight and the gun was there. He wasn't holding it

217

then. I think he put it on his lap by then. That's where I remember reaching for it, and as I got up, I grabbed for the gun and Hy dropped the phone and he grabbed my wrist and I pulled back and he let go and I went back on the other bed. I fell back the way you would in a tug-of-war and Hy lunged forward at me, as though he were going to tackle me, and his hands came out like that, around my waist, and there was an instant when I felt the muzzle of the gun in my stomach. I thought it was the muzzle of the gun, and I had the gun in my hand and I pulled the trigger and it exploded again, with such a loud sound, and my first thought was: My God, that didn't hurt at all, I should have done it a long time ago. And then Hy fell back and I got up and ran.

Aurnou: Why did you run?

Harris: Because I wanted to get far enough away from him to shoot myself before he caught me again.

Aurnou: Where did you run to?

Harris: I ran from where we were between the beds around his bed, and I got almost up near the end of his bed, I thought right near that closet. Near the edge of the closet between the bathroom and the closet is where I thought I was. I stopped right about there.

Aurnou: Where was Hy then?

Harris: He was down—he was on his knees, actually, between the beds, and that he wasn't chasing me was what was important to me.

Aurnou: What did you do?

Harris: I stopped there at the head of the bed near the closet and I put the gun to my head and I took a very deep breath and I pulled the trigger and the gun clicked.

Aurnou: You mean it fired?

Harris: No, it didn't fire, and I had gone to great

pains to see that that couldn't happen, and I tried to think of an adjective for that too.

Aurnou: What did you do next?

Harris: I heard the gun and I looked at it, because I couldn't see—I was sure I loaded it, Joel, with six bullets, and I thought there were a lot of bullets left, and I looked at it and I pulled the trigger and it exploded, and I thought it had gone possibly back into the rug. I found out months later, as you know, that it had gone into the cupboard right next to the headboard. And I put it back up to my head and I shot and I shot and I shot and I shot and I shot and it just clicked, and Suzanne and Henri hadn't been heard from, but part of the panic was thinking, "God, they'll be here any minute," and the gun was either not working or it was empty, or I had to find some more bullets for it, because I wanted to get more bullets in it and be dead before Suzanne and Henri got up there, and I know I had put some bullets in my pocket when I filled the gun. I haven't any idea how many I put in, and I looked for my coat and I couldn't find it. I ran around the room, and finally I found it on the floor next to the television set. I don't remember taking it off or putting it there, but that's where I found it, and I took it into the bathroom and I emptied the pocket on the floor and there were some bullets in it.

Aurnou: Was there anything else in your pocket that emptied out on the floor?

Harris: I didn't know, at that time. I saw some change in the picture, but I don't remember that. And I pulled out the cylinder and again tried to pull out the shells and they didn't move. So I banged the gun on the tub and they didn't move. So I banged it on the tub again and they didn't move, and I think I banged it a third time and I banged it very hard and

219

it flew out of my hand and went into the bathtub, and I leaned over and picked it up and it was broken. When it fell into the bathtub, the cylinder part wasn't part of the gun anymore. It had broken. It was the crane. I heard the word. I don't know. It broke the thing that attached to the rest of the gun.

So I spent a frantic—I don't know how long. I suppose a minute or seconds, minutes, and tried to put the cylinder back into the gun, and I got it part way and almost all the way in, but I couldn't really line it up, and finally I walked back into Hy's room and I saw him just dropping the phone—not the whole phone, the receiver, and he turned and he was pulling himself up on my bed and he obviously hadn't gotten an outside line yet, and I went over and I picked up the phone and I listened and heard nothing. There wasn't a buzz, there wasn't anything. And I pushed the thing and nothing happened, and I put it back down on the hook and I said, "Hy, it's broken. I think it's gone dead," and Hy said, "You're probably right." That was the only civil thing he said all night, and that was the last thing I heard him say. And he pulled himself up and he leaned on me and he went back over toward his bed and I helped him back on to the bed, and when I left Hy, he was lying on a blue velour blanket near the head of the—near the foot of the bed, and when he went back, his hands both went out, and he looked exhausted, but he didn't look dying. His color looked—I looked at his face and he looked at me and I guess we were both in a state of shock, wondering how something could— how something that ugly and sad could have happened between two people who didn't argue, even, except over the use of the subjunctive, and I ran downstairs and I ran to the front door, and when I got there, the light was on in the dining room, and the door that Henri and Suzanne usually had closed in the dining room was open, and I could hear Suzanne's voice. She was in the dining room, but I didn't see her.

She was talking to someone and I got to the door and it was all dark in the foyer and on the steps, and it has another one of those turn switches, and I saw it and I said, "Somebody turn on the goddamn lights, I'm going for help," and I pushed something and the light went on. I'm not sure which one it was, but I could see my way down the steps and I ran down, leaving the door wide open, and I got in the car, and I headed toward the Community Center where I knew there was a phone.

Aurnou: How far away was that?

Harris: I don't know how far. I know it's exactly one mile to Anderson Hill Road, because Hy wrote that on the first instructions he wrote me on how to get there, but I don't know—I guess it's about half a mile to the Community Center. I don't know.

Aurnou: As you got into the Community Center parking lot, what if anything happened?

Harris: I turned in and drove up toward the phone booth. You can see it easily. It has a light on it. And I looked up and I could see off to the right the Anderson Hill light and I saw a police car coming with flashing lights, and when I saw it, I didn't get out of the car, I backed around and I turned back and headed back to Hy's house. I got almost to his driveway and I thought, "My God, maybe they are not coming to his house, maybe they are going to the airport or something." But I went into the driveway, and by the time I got to the toolshed, I could see the lights following behind me.

Aurnou: Had the policeman given you any sign or any signal of any kind indicating that you were to stop

221

or follow him or do any particular thing?

Harris: No. He didn't know where he was when he followed me into the driveway. I think he followed me in because he was going to ask me how to get to where he was supposed to go. I got out of my car, and the policeman, whom I now know to be McKenna, didn't get out of his. He was listening, I guess, to his radio, he said. I ran over to his car and I can remember shouting, "Hurry up, hurry up." I don't know whether I said, "Hurry, he's been shot, please, hurry up, hurry up," and I ran up the steps with McKenna behind me, and Henri was standing at the top of the steps silhouetted against the front door. He was outside of the front door and he was screaming hysterically, "She's the one, she did it, she's the one," and I ran into the house and Suzanne was somewhere inside the foyer and we ran upstairs. I believe Suzanne ran up first. I ran next. I know McKenna came up last. And I got to Hy's bedroom—

Aurnou: Did Henri come up at that time at all?

Harris: No. He didn't come up until another policeman came. And Hy was on the floor lying on his back between the two beds.

Aurnou: When you first got back there, Hy was on the floor on his back lying between the two beds?

Harris: Yes. He was right exactly where McKenna described him in his police report that night, though it's not what he said to the jury when he came here.

Aurnou: Who was in that room when you got back to the house, you or McKenna?

Harris: I was there before McKenna.

Aurnou: Did anyone get in that room before you did?

Harris: Suzanne says that she ran up before we got there. I don't know. She may have been up there before.

Aurnou: When you came back to the house with McKenna, in what order did anyone go upstairs?

Harris: Suzanne and I went upstairs and McKenna came up in back of us.

Aurnou: How long did McKenna stay?

Harris: He just looked at Hy and ran back down for his oxygen equipment.

Aurnou: Was Henri there then?

Harris: No. Suzanne and Hy and I were in the room for at least a moment alone. At least as long as it took for McKenna to run down and get his oxygen.

Aurnou: What did Suzanne do?

Harris: Suzanne went over and knelt on the floor beside him and took his hand and spoke to him very gently, and I lay across the bed and leaned over and caressed his face and talked to him, too.

Aurnou: What did you say?

Harris: I said, "Oh, Hy, why didn't you kill me?" I couldn't figure out why he was on the floor when I left him on the bed, and then I looked up and saw the receiver from the phone dangling down. Everybody else had said it was on the floor, but I remember very clearly it being up on the shelf and the receiver hanging down and covered with blood, and I realized Hy had gotten up and gone over and tried to phone again, and then fallen back. He was trying to talk to us then, too, but he couldn't speak, and not three minutes before he spoke perfectly clearly.

Aurnou: Mrs. Harris, when you left the house to go to the telephone to get help, did you know how many bullets, or how many bullets did you think had actually been fired in that room?

Harris: Well, I knew that I had now shot all the way around it. They must have all been shot. I knew of three shots. I knew of the one in his hand, I knew of the one when I thought I shot myself in the stomach, and I knew of the one that I shot into space or the floor or wherever it landed, but it wasn't anywhere near Hy.

Aurnou: Have you thought since then of when the other two shots were fired?

Bolen: Objection. I object.

The Court: I am sustaining the objection as to the form. You can ask her whether she knows now.

Aurnou: Have you made any effort in your mind since March 10 to recall the events of that night?

Harris: I spent eleven months thinking about it, Joel. I know when the first shot was fired and I know when the last shot was fired and I know that I shot at myself, I thought, when we were there between the beds, and I know the only time Hy and I were close together struggling for the gun was in that minute or so between the beds when I grabbed for the gun and he grabbed for my arm, and it had to be in that period of time. I don't know—when he grabbed my hand, it's possible it went off then. I believe when I fell back, it went off then, but I did not know when I left Hy that night the first time or the second time when the police made me go downstairs, I did not know that he had been shot any place except in the hand, and that was the only place I saw bleeding ever, and he was not, as Mr. McKenna changed his mind, and as Henri changed his mind for this jury, on his knees with blood pouring out his back. There was very little blood near Hy. The only thing that really bled was his hand, and he was lying on his back. McKenna saw a chest wound. I didn't see that. But I really only remember looking at his face and touching his face when I came back.

Aurnou: Mrs. Harris, after you lay across the bed, stroked the doctor's face, talked to him, what happened then?

224

Harris: Well, McKenna came back up first with some oxygen and put it over Hy's face, and very shortly thereafter another policeman came up and that was when Henri came up, too, and the other policeman told me I had to come downstairs, and I asked him to please let me stay with Hy and he said, "You can't, you have to come down," and I got up and went downstairs with him, and I believe Henri and Suzanne came down then, too.

Aurnou: At any time that night did you intend to harm Hy?

Harris: No, I did not, ever, ever, not for one instant.

Aurnou: Did you ever that night intend to shoot or kill Dr. Tarnower?

Harris: No, I didn't. The most violent thing I did was throw a box of curlers, and I didn't throw them at him. I never for a moment wanted to hurt Hy, never in fourteen years, and certainly not that night.

2.

Hy was taken to the hospital and died there at 11:58 P.M., March 10, 1980. Shortly thereafter I was arrested and brought to the Harrison police station. I spent the rest of that night in the Harrison jail, in a small cage, guarded by a kind woman who did what she could to make it easier for me. I remember it as a long night when I didn't feel anything at all, no concern about me, little awareness of Hy's death. The next day I was moved to the jail in Valhalla, and the following morning my sisters, Mary Margaret Lynch and Virginia McLaughlin, and my brother Robert Struven flew in from all over the country and bailed me out.

From Valhalla I was taken to the mental ward of the United Hospital in Portchester, where I stayed for ten days. I had always had a good feeling about Portchester, without knowing anything about it. In the years that I drove from Philadelphia to see Hy, Portchester meant I was almost there. I will always remember the kindness of the women on the mental ward floor. I welcomed the idea of going there. I wanted a world with women in crisp white uniforms and sheets pulled tight. It sounded safe. Instead, I arrived to find everyone in slacks and tee shirts, nurses as well as patients. It was all very informal, the way, I'm told, most mental patients respond the best. Not I.

"My God," I cried, "I don't know which are the nurses and which are the patients. Get me out of here." I had been told that I wasn't being "committed," that I could leave if I wanted to, but by the time I realized that I wanted to leave, the doors were locked and no one was quite sure who had the key. Finally, they quieted me with a shot of something, and I slept for twenty-four hours.

When I awoke, the volunteer on the floor came in to talk with me. She was out of slacks and wearing a suit. Five days later she said to me most kindly, "Mrs. Harris, I know you were upset by all the people in slacks when you came in, but slacks are what I usually live and work in. I'm running out of skirts. Would it upset you now if I went back to slacks?" In every possible way, both staff and volunteers did what they could to help a desperately sad and shaken woman. For ten days the media banged on doors trying to find out where I was, and no one told them.

I was allowed to use the public phone there on the floor, and I used it only once, to call Hy. White

Plains nine, eight, three, eight, nine had been my lifeline for a very long time. I felt a physical need to dial it. Suzanne van der Vreken answered the phone. She cried and so did I. Then she said, "Oh madame, it is so sad. They say I cannot speak with you again." That was the last time I heard the woman I had known as Hy's cook and housekeeper for fourteen years, the one who had given me one of her paintings when I left for Virginia, and which Henri had framed for me. When I saw her again on the witness stand at my trial, she had become a total stranger, describing a woman I never was.

Using all the physical and mental powers at my disposal during those ten days in the hospital I managed to play solitaire, stare into space, sleep, and weep. I couldn't read or write for many weeks. Suicide was still much the best, much the most logical choice. Part of that ten days was spent taking psychological tests. I found it difficult to take them. I didn't want to have to talk that much or think that much. The tests were administered then and later by Dr. Eileen Bloomingdale, a forensic psychologist, and, I believe, a very wise woman. The first test she gave me was a Wechsler Intelligence Test, a basic IQ.

The hardest part for me was forgetting words, simple words and simple facts. I couldn't remember who wrote Faust and that bothered me. At the time it seemed terribly important to me that I remember it. I tried playing games with the doctor, "I'll tell you how the story in the picture ends if you'll just tell me who wrote Faust." She wrote a great deal later about my "need to be in control." I thought then, and I think now that it was control of me I wanted, not of others. Finding answers that made sense to me and satisfied me has used a lot of ergs of my energy over a lifetime.

I'm afraid the thing that frightened me most about

the tests was the very real threat that they would discover I wasn't intelligent and then everyone would know. I could imagine my IQ in a *New York Post* headline. I had functioned as a reasonably intelligent person for a long time, but maybe it was just something I had gotten the hang of, a part I had played, and right down at rock bottom the truth was I didn't have too many marbles.

There are two parts to a Wechsler Intelligence Test, one verbal, one performance. One thing I was absolutely sure of was that my verbal score would be higher than my performance (putting puzzles together, matching, this is to this as that is to what). The other thing I was sure of from long years of studying student IQs was that a twenty point difference between verbal and performance scores usually meant something was amiss and the student in question could profit from some psychological counseling, because a gap that wide did signify some lack of balance.

As it turned out my performance score was twenty-three points higher than my verbal. I could put the puzzle together like nobody's business, but I couldn't remember words. As for my IQ, it turned out to be high enough so that the *New York Post* wouldn't have any fun printing it.

The Wechsler Intelligence Test was followed by the Rorschach Inkblot Test, the Bender Gestalt drawing of shapes, Benton Visual Recall, Minnesota Multiphasic Personality Inventory, and Thematic Apperception Tests. Later, when two EEGs indicated "dysfunction of the brain when not in resting position," "definite abnormalities when hyperventilating," I went back for more tests; the Goldstein-Scherer Sorting Test, Halstead-Deiton Trailmaking Test, Lurea Nebraska Neuro Psychology

Test. They didn't explain the EEG, and I was assured by the neurologist who poked and prodded me that all my reflexes are normal, that the brain is a mystery, and they will probably never explain my EEG.

When I left the hospital, there was still a houseful of my worldly possessions sitting in the headmistress' house down in McLean, Virginia. David, my son, drove me there the next day, and in nineteen hours we had packed everything and were gone. Not one member of the Board came to see me. One called. The School motto, "Function in disaster, finish in style" is for the students—and the headmistress.

The months between Hy's death in March of 1980 and the beginning of the pre-trial in October still have a quality of unreality about them. They were quiet and lonely and private and sad. I walked the dog and went to the psychiatrist, and read and wrote, and sat alone in a bedroom in a kind friend's house. Within a few hours after Hy's death, and the public announcement that Joel Aurnou would be my lawyer, Frances Baxton called his office and left the message that if I were not allowed to leave Westchester, I was welcome to stay with her.

Frances's husband, Carter Braxton, had only recently had a stroke. He was still in the hospital. Hy was his doctor. In fact, the last professional visit of his life was to Carter in White Plains Hospital.

We were a strange household: Frances with her cats, I with Cider, my golden retriever, and poor desperately ill Carter. When he came home from the hospital there were nurses for him almost around the clock, but not from 5:00 in the evening to 11:00. Nights when Frances went out were the only times I did anything remotely useful. I fed Carter and bathed him, and brought him whatever I could figure out he might want. I never knew exactly how much he understood about what I was doing there. Sometimes when I tried to explain, he held my hand very tight. Other times he just stared into space.

Other than those evenings alone, my only contact with Carter was bringing him flowers from the garden. I picked them for him and arranged them in his room. I picked them for Hy too, and brought them to his grave. And then finally, it was October, and while I moved into the courtroom to live, Cider moved into Carter's room to keep him company. I think Carter became fond of her.

My only real connection to the outside world during those long months were the letters I received, hundreds and hundreds of them from old friends, classmates, students, students' parents, fellow teachers, people for whom I had worked, and people who had worked for me. Before the trial began almost four hundred people had written offering to be character witnesses for me. I didn't know until later that character is of no consequence in a courtroom. The kindness of the letters reduced me to deep, wracking sobs. It was often hours after they had arrived before I could finish reading them.

Many of the girls at Madeira wrote wonderful letters, kind and remarkably sensitive in what was an unthinkable situation for them as well as for me. The seniors dedicated their yearbook to me. They had voted to do it long before, but they took another vote after Hy's death, and they still dedicated it to me. They could have changed it but they didn't. This note came with the yearbook when it arrived. How could I ever tell them what it meant?

Dear Mrs. Harris,

On behalf of the Senior Class, the *Epilogue*, and the rest of the Madeira community we would like to present you with this year's annual. We have worked long and hard on the book and we hope that you like it. We have carefully chosen to dedicate the book to a very special lady we respect, admire, and love very much. We feel strongly that she is quite worthy of this honor. This year's *Epilogue* is proudly dedicated to you. Unfortunately it is only a small recognition of an appreciation of you and all you have done for Madeira. The dedication comes from the bottom of our hearts. We truly miss you and hope the very best for you. Thank you for all your support of the *Epilogue* this past school year. We hope that you enjoy the book.

Sincerely,

The very first letter to arrive followed a telegram to Joel saying, "If there's anything I can do I will come at once." It was from a young woman who lives in Denver and whom I hadn't seen or heard from since she graduated from the Thomas school five years before. She wrote, "I'm not sure you ever really knew what kind of influence you had on me. You changed my life at Thomas, from being a wandering minstrel to being a responsible, productive human being. I knew what you expected just by the air you had about you, and I think by graduation day I had begun to prove to you, my family and myself what I had to offer the world." At the end she wrote, "I hope you will be able to find a new dimension in your life and receive some profit from what you have invested in other people's lives."

Some well meaning friends believed what they had

231

read in the papers and wrote, "Whatever you did I forgive you." That is not a sentence to gladden the heart, whether it comes from a child, a friend, or a stranger. Two of the girls from Madeira, in all innocence and kindness wrote, "No matter what you did I love you and forgive you." I was deeply troubled by these and answered them with long philosophical treatises on how I hoped they had faith in my innocence, but if they thought I had murdered someone they hadn't the right to forgive me.

One old classmate of forty years ago wrote what I am sure she meant in all kindness. She remembered that I used to swing my leg nervously in Miss Andrew's English class and was relegated to a back seat for it. She remembered that I was always "taut as a wire" and that I always had "very high standards for yourself and for others." From that she had deduced that now, forty years later, I must be capable of murder—and anyway she almost did her husband in when he walked off with his secretary, so the whole thing would be logical and forgivable.

What she didn't seem to know, and indeed what the media didn't acknowledge and the District Attorney forgot, is that loving an old bachelor is always a no-win situation, and you come to terms with that early on, or you go away. It may be a shock when you find that love letter or motel key in a husband's pocket, but you don't go through pockets to find a bachelor's other women. He brings them all home. A little scarf, a little earring, a little curler, even with his trusty "house manager" hiding it all as best she could. It's always there. If you are honest with yourself you never indulge in the luxury of thinking that you're needed. I wrote to Hy years ago, "I wish I had been a doormat or a man instead of the miserable half-breed I've turned out to be. I want very much to feel like your equal, but love is no equalizer."

There were letters from women, most of them friends, some strangers, all of them wishing me well and then bursting into the story of their own sad lives. Letters from men usually came later. It was harder for men to write than for women. Women are less self-conscious about tragedy, more at home with it. I loved the letter that came in September from one of the men I had worked with in New York at Allied Maintenance:

"My thoughts and opinion of you are the same as when we worked together. I admired your honesty, competence, dedication, and sharp humor. You always seemed to be on the "up" side of things, and could see the day and the work through, this in spite of everybody else. I am hesitant to ask How are you?, but, well, How are you? Are you going to see the day through with your high standards of respect and competency? I hope so."

Old friends wrote very personal and loving notes:

"Remember when Carl was dying and you came and cut the front lawn and edged the garden?"

"Remember the shake-down cruise of the *Galetea* and you and Dee Dee and Liz insisted it was a put-down to be called "the girls" so from then on we called you "the former girls?" Remember? Remember, Remember?

Teachers wrote:

"The campus is beautiful and each time I stop as I walk across the campus I think of every flower you have caused to be planted. A daffodil in bloom anywhere this spring has reminded me of you."

"I've thought of your pain. Yes, I've thought of that quite a lot. I can't imagine that you have room in your personal structure for sympathy, and the inherent limitations on presuming to empathize. . . . I don't know the word, if there is one that expresses my awareness of you, my belief in you as a person, and my belief in those qualities of living which you have instilled in so many of the girls and the faculty."

Heads of schools wrote:

"I know that you have the strength to get through this rough time. I remember how strong you were in the Thomas School situation, and I prize your years at Madeira. That superb Harris intelligence and humor brought a refreshingly open atmosphere to an old and solid school."

"Because I, like many of your colleagues, have known and admired you as a capable and delightful person, we have come to love and admire you. . . . Life certainly can take matters out of what we consider our capable and decisive hands."

Students, bless them, wrote:

"I want you to do as you once told me, rest, eat well, and keep your spirits up. We've both worked hard this year and we're going to make it."

"I remember when you helped me through a very difficult time in my life . . . you always seemed to have a moment to talk and ask me how things were going."

"I've written you two letters before but I was too embarrassed to send them. One was about a beautiful speech you gave at chapel about a month ago. You talked about getting to know people, giving them a chance, even if they live in a different 'box.' That hit home. I realized how many doors I had closed to myself. I'm enjoying getting to know people I thought were 'nice' but a little strange."

"Much love to a dear lady. Don't worry about us. We'll make it. We love you."

Westchester:
The People of
New York State vs.
Jean Harris

On October 15, 1980, the first contingent of potential jurors gathered in the large auditorium at the Westchester courthouse. Ordinarily a pool of four hundred citizens are notified to report for jury duty. For the Harris trial one thousand people were notified. Judge Russell Leggett who was to preside over the case introduced himself, the lawyers—Joel Aurnou for the defense, Assistant District Attorney George Bolen for the prosecution—and the defendant Jean Harris. He read the three charges for which I was indicted: count one, murder in the second degree, count two, criminal possession of a weapon, in the state of New York, second degree, and count three, criminal possession of a weapon in a place not the defendant's home or place of business, third degree.

The judge then gave a dignified pep talk about the American system of justice. "You will be," he charged them, "judges of the fact. You are the sole and exclusive judges of what the truth is. You will bring with you here your common sense. Without your common sense you defeat the purpose of your being here. You are fact finders, and as such you decide credibility. Your verdict will be 'Guilty' or

'Not Guilty.' Your job is not to find innocence." I still don't fully understand that.

Judge Legget continued. "This case comes here by way of an indictment in Westchester. An indictment is of no evidential value—it simply lists charges—you cannot decide guilt because of an indictment—the defendant is presumed innocent until proven guilty. Our jury system is the greatest bastion for justice that has ever been devised by the minds of men. You must come in with a fair and impartial mind—no predjudice or sympathy—sympathy has no place here. The burden of proof is upon the people. They must convince you, beyond a reasonable doubt of the defendant's guilt, or you are obliged to find her not guilty. You do not need to be given proof beyond all possible doubt, only beyond 'reasonable' doubt." What is a reasonable doubt was to become the best kept secret of the trial.

"Reasonable doubt," the judge explained, "really gets down to common sense and your own home-grown intuition. What you happen to think because of your interpretation of the facts as you see them."

When the Harris trial is mentioned, even today, the first question is usually "Why didn't she plead extreme emotional disturbance, EED?" The answer is simple. My lawyers didn't recommend it, and their explanation of EED given to me, during the trial and the three years after the trial was always, "If you want to plead EED you have to first say that you murdered Hy, but you did it under extreme emotional disturbance."

Again and again I protested the same way. "But that's Catch 22. It doesn't make any sense. You're telling me that the way to be acquitted of murder is to say that I murdered a man. I didn't murder Hy, and nothing and no one will ever induce me to say that I did." It was always the same conversation, with the same advice, and the same frustrated answer from me. Joel said it was probably a lucky break that I was indicted for murder because there was "No way in hell anyone could find you guilty of murder." He worked very hard to make that be true, but it didn't happen.

Picking a jury is a complicated, frightening business—so much is at stake. At the initial screening all the questions were put by the judge. Some people were excused "for cause," some were asked to return November 1, by which time Judge Leggett thought the formal voir dire would begin. If there were no obvious "cause" for dismissal and the two lawyers disagreed about a candidate, Judge Leggett decided whether to dismiss or ask the person to return. What caused one or the other lawyers to object to something was sometimes obvious, sometimes not. It could be a gut feeling, or merely the other lawyer's enthusiasm. Good poker players have an edge here.

I had no idea how long and how grim the screening of jurors could be. Each session seemed interminable. Next to Suzanne van der Vreken's testimony and Bolen's summation, screening of jurors was for me the most traumatic part of the whole endless ordeal. I was unprepared for the ugliness, still believing as I did that my life spoke well of me. "Everyone knows she's a murderer. Why should I give my time to serve on a jury for her?" "This whole trial is a farce. It's just a big expensive game to promote legal careers." On the third day of screening I passed this note to Joel.

"Joel, is it required by law that I sit through this? If it is not, I wish to leave."

Joel wrote, "Why?"

I answered, "I am totally disinterested in who gets

237

on the jury. I consider the trial over."

He looked annoyed, and wrote, "That is nonsense. Please allow me to concentrate on the proceedings."

There were lighter moments, though not very many. My presence inhibited many people who felt obliged to search for appropriate euphemisms to describe what they thought was my relationship to Dr. Tarnower. "I know there was something between them that went beyond the normal course of friendship." "They had a, you know, an adult relationship." "Well of course I understand. My son is divorced now, so he's just a consenting adult too." "I read that they had been—that they had a relationship." "I only know she was supposed to be with him—you know—with him." When a brash young woman breezed in and was asked if she could be impartial in judging Mrs. Harris, she replied, "After the life she's led, I certainly couldn't." Judge Leggett, feeling that perhaps the girl was going too far in judging my morality or lack of it, made some comment to that effect. "Oh," she said, "I don't think she's immoral. I think she's an idiot!" I wrote Joel a hasty note: "I can make a case for that. Let's take her." But she was dismissed for cause.

An elderly candidate had the story confused, but no qualms at all about speaking his mind. "I have a personal reason that keeps me from being impartial," he said. "My niece took up with a married man. I have strong moral feelings." Leggett asked, "Would moral disagreement make it hard for you to be impartial? Could you decide on the facts?" He answered, "I would try, except I feel deeply it led to this situation."

Knowing of the long Tryforos affair with Dr. Tarnower, George Bolen turned to his assistant Tom Lalla and said, a little too loud, "I'm not sure which

way he's going. I thing he should go for cause."
Having never "taken up with a married man," I
shared the man's strong moral convictions. I wanted
to keep him. He too was excused for cause.

Another candidate said, "I read in two papers
quite a bit. I'm very much in favor of the poor guy
who got killed. I'm in favor of the death penalty."
After this Leggett asked, "But would you have trouble being fair to both sides?" It's in the record!

Because of the notoriety of the case some people
were obviously torn between their personal obliga-
tions and thinking it might be "fun" to get involved.
The more eager they seemed, the less eager either
lawyer was to have them. One woman, obviously a
detective story buff, said she would be "enchanted"
to serve, but first she had to clear up one question.
Leaning over toward the judge because she felt embarrassed that I might hear her, she stage whispered,
"Where did they actually find the gun? If I know
that, I think I've solved the whole thing."

The overwhelming influence of the press on the
jury and the eventual outcome of the trial was immediately obvious. Potential jurors walked into the
courtroom carrying under their arms newspapers that
screamed, "Officer Testifies Mrs. H Said She was
Slayer." "She Told Me Harris Shot Dr." "Diet Doc's
Girl Hopes to Die with Her Lover." "Police allege she
had written certain notes indicating she was going to
commit this murder." Not one single paper reported
that there was no confession of murder. Of almost
four-hundred people finally screened by Judge Leggett, there were fewer than ten who had not heard
about the case through the media.

Prospective jurors went on interminably about
what they read in the press:

"I read about the case in the papers. The doctor

239

was alone. I think everything was pretty obvious."

"Have you made up your mind if the defendant is guilty?"

"Yes."

"Based on what you've read in the papers?"

"Yes."

"I'd have trouble separating what I've read and what I hear in court."

"I've read about the case and formed an opinion."

"I've read everything in the paper. I've half formed an opinion. It would be a little hard to forget what I've learned. I think I would be confused."

"I have definite feelings about the case. This woman came up and shot the man . . . let her . . . why should we take all that time being on a jury?"

"I've read about it. I really don't know if I could be impartial about it. She shot him in a rage."

Page after page of such comments accumulated as the screening went on. By October 27 Judge Leggett had asked 106 women and 81 men to return for the formal voir dire. "I am convinced," he said, "that all those who have been asked back are able to be impartial." A number of those asked back had even questioned their own ability to be impartial. Four of Hy's acquaintances were asked to return, as was a woman whose family was, in her words, "best friends with his sister, Mrs. Pearl ("Billie") Schwartz."

Joel Aurnou thought long and hard about a change of venue out of Westchester for the trial. But by October, there were in his office three large volumes of national newspaper and magazine clippings covering the case. There was no place to move to in New York State, or even any other state if that had been an option, where the story of the "Diet Doc and the aging mistress" had not been headlined and reported in the most lurid terms. The trial remained in West-